HUMILITY

HUMILITY

Norvin Richards

Temple University Press
Philadelphia

Temple University Press, Philadelphia 19122
Copyright © 1992 by Temple University. All rights reserved
Published 1992
Printed in the United States of America

The paper used in this publication meets the minimum requirements of
American National Standard for Information Sciences—Permanence of Paper
for Printed Library Materials, ANSI Z39.48-1984 ⊗

Library of Congress Cataloging-in-Publication Data
    Richards, Norvin, 1943-
        Humility / Norvin Richards.
            p.   cm.
        Includes bibliographical references.
        ISBN 0-87722-927-9 (hard)
        1. Humility.   I. Title.
    BJ1533.H93R53   1992
    179'.9—dc20   92-3110

To Thelma Richards, without whose love I would never have become the person I am, and to Janet Richards, whose love makes me happy that I did

CONTENTS

ACKNOWLEDGMENTS

I am grateful to a number of people who have read or listened to parts of this and provided helpful suggestions. These include Glenn Allen, Joan Callahan, W. R. Carter, Max Hocutt, Bruce Kimball, Ralph Perhac, George Rainbolt, Norvin Richards III, Mark Rowlands, and Casey Swank. My thanks also to the anonymous reviewer employed by Temple, whose suggestions improved the manuscript considerably, and to Debby Stuart, also of Temple, whose editing so improved its prose.

I owe debts of much longer standing to the late José Franquiz and to Joe Mow, who opened the door to philosophy and encouraged me to enter; to the philosophy faculty of the University of Virginia, who provided me a way of defining and approaching philosophical questions that has been richly satisfying; and especially to George Thomas, whose clarity of mind and intellectual integrity remain my aspirations.

The *American Philosophical Quarterly* kindly granted permission to use "Is Humility a Virtue?" (July 1988) as the heart of Chapter 1. I am also indebted to Max Hocutt for his confidence and support; to Genevieve, Norvin, and Janet Richards for their unfailing love and confidence; to Genevieve

Richards for help with the Index and with reading proof; to George McClure and Phil Beidler for suggesting scholarly and literary sources on which to draw; and, finally, to Scott Hestevold, who has read every word and discussed with me every idea offered here, always to my great benefit, and without whose conversation this book would have been far poorer and the writing of it nowhere near so enjoyable.

INTRODUCTION

Those who lecture on Aristotle's ethics come eventually to the person of *megalopsuchia*, the paragon who shines in every virtue and is perfectly aware of this glorious fact. To convey what such a person would be like, Renford Bambrough customarily offers the late Lord Mountbatten. Bambrough recounts his hero's many virtues, then ends with a flourish: "and there was none of this damned *humility* about the man."

Bambrough's flourish has considerable effect on those listeners who have always thought of humility as a good thing, perhaps even a *very* good thing. And yet, if humility amounts to having a low opinion of oneself, how *could* someone who knew he had all the virtues be humble? Indeed, how could someone even well supplied with virtues or accomplishments think that he was nothing much? His mistake would be so obvious that it would seem more plausible to suspect he was being insincere. Could the truth be that it is always *false* humility we find in the accomplished, never the real thing? That would certainly be ironic, since it is the humility of the especially accomplished that impresses us the most: "To have done all that and still be so humble," we marvel. "Isn't she remarkable?"

Then again, suppose the accomplished person's humility were genuine: not a repellent pretense, that is, but the genuine article. If this is a matter of her honest opinion of herself being a poor one, why would it be a *good thing* about her? It sounds more like something we should want to help her repair than like something we should admire. If humility is only a species of inaccuracy, why is it a virtue? More generally, how is it distinguishable from a lack of proper self-respect? Martin Luther believed humility is so wonderful that no humble person could ever be aware of being humble, because the awareness would surely turn his head.[1] Once one stops to think about it, however, it begins to seem more pitiful than admirable.

In Chapter 1 I argue that humility is dubious in these ways only if we persist in equating it with having a low opinion of oneself, or with underestimating oneself. Granted, those are the usual ways to picture humility. I argue for a different analysis, however, according to which being humble is not a matter of thinking poorly of oneself but (roughly) a matter of having oneself in perspective. On this view, humility consists in understanding oneself and what one has done too clearly to be inclined to exaggeration. It is not a matter of thinking that one's accomplishments and virtues come literally to naught, but just of esteeming them no more highly than they deserve.

That is not always easy to manage, given culturally encouraged yearnings to be exceptional and (for some) exaggerated praise for what they have done. It is easy to lose perspective. Those who keep it have something that it is not implausible to consider a virtue, it seems. Thus, on this account it is not puzzling why humility should be admirable, unlike the account on which humility consists in underestimating oneself or in thinking badly of oneself.

Nor is there reason to think a talented and accomplished person would be too wise and knowledgeable to have herself in perspective, as there is to think she would be too wise and knowledgeable to underestimate herself or to have a genuinely poor opinion of herself. So humility changes to something an impressive person *could* have, just as we would like to believe. Moreover, it does seem especially admirable that such a person should have retained her perspective despite her many fine points, whereas it only seems especially *sad* for her to think poorly of herself in spite of them. That is another reason to think of humility as perspective, rather than as thinking badly of oneself.

In short, I argue in Chapter 1, "Is Humility a Virtue?" that certain philosophical puzzles are solved, if we think of humility differently than we might be accustomed to doing. Fair enough, perhaps, but this tells us little about how our lives would be affected if we were humble. How would your compassion for others be affected, for example, if you had yourself and your accomplishments in proper perspective? Would it incline you to abandon your usual pursuits and work full time for famine relief? Would it have some less dramatic effect? Answering this sort of question reveals what humility actually comes to, it seems to me, and I devote the balance of the book to doing so.

That project begins with something that is some part of everyone's life: mistreatment at the hands of others, and how to react to it. We are all wronged, on occasion, though we differ in how grievously and how regularly we are. We also differ greatly in how we react to being wronged, both in our initial responses and in our later inclinations to forgive, to carry a grudge, or to seek revenge. As Jeffrie Murphy has lately emphasized, in some reactions to mistreatment there is a lack of self-respect.[2] However, it is also possible to exaggerate the importance of being mistreated, and thereby to exaggerate one's own importance. The question in Chapter 2, "Mistreatment," is how *humility* would affect one, in this regard.

Chapter 3, "Compassion," turns from mistreatment to claims upon one's fellow-feeling. The world is richly supplied with people who are suffering miserably. We know that, and we could help them. To do so, however, would interfere with our other projects, to a greater or lesser degree. How seriously should we take those projects, in light of their suffering? How seriously should we take their suffering, in the light of our projects? What does a proper humility require, by way of compassion?

Just as the world contains many who are far worse off than we, it also contains many who are far better off. And not just better off materially, though there are plenty of those. There are also people who just have richer and fuller and happier lives than we do. There are people who are more talented, people who are better read and more wise, people who are more kind and brave and true, and so on. It is possible to admire our various betters, or even to be happy for them. But it is also possible to envy them, or to be jealous, even to be *consumed* by such feelings.

These reactions are the subject of Chapter 4, "Envy and Jealousy." The question is how humility would dispose a person, in this regard. Would it be proof against these reactions, which have a certain competitiveness to them? Or, would humility free a person from some forms of envy and jealousy but not from others? Or would the effect be just the opposite: are the humble actually more *inclined* to resent those who are doing better than they?

We come next to paternalism, the effort to influence or control the lives of others for their own good. There is a presumptuousness about paternalism that we might expect to repel a person of humility, an element of interfering in something that may be none of our business. And yet, all of us are powerfully inclined to look after those for whom we have affectionate concern: that is part of caring for them, it seems. Moreover, caring for others is part of being unabsorbed in oneself. So a humble person *ought* to care for others—but, somehow, without imposing herself on them. Perhaps there is paternalism that humility endorses or even prescribes, as well as paternalism in which we arrogantly overstep ourselves. These matters are taken up in Chapter 5, "Paternalism and Arrogance."

In addition to acting paternalistically ourselves, there is also the question of responding to the paternalistic attentions of others. Does self-respect demand that we resist? Is resistance ever a failure of humility? Chapter 6, "It's My Life!" approaches this through the example of major medical decisions, where it might be thought unhumble to resist professional advice or to insist that loved ones must bear the cost of one's choice.

Whether this resistance or insistence truly is unhumble depends on what it is for something to be a particular person's life, I argue. That is the basis for a person's interests in shaping that life, and those interests turn out to be quite powerful. This means it is mostly *not* a failure of humility to assert one's autonomy, I contend. On the other hand, lives can be so intertwined that a decision cannot shape one life without also shaping another. Then it can be unhumble to insist on having things one's own way, I argue, and I offer some ideas about resolving such dilemmas.

Finally, is it reasonable to expect that a humble person would live simply, with a minimum of possessions? The association seems natural enough: think of a humble dwelling, humble fare, a person of humble means. How *would* humility incline us, in the matter of worldly goods? In Chapter 7, "The Simple Life," I consider this question. I draw first on arguments offered by various fathers of the Catholic church, then on arguments that inform the Amish way of life, then on arguments independent of any particular tradition. These discussions provide the opportunity to think not only about whether humility would incline a person to live simply but also about what humility has to do with ambition, with boastfulness, and with modesty.

In the final chapter, "The Virtue of Humility," I draw together these separate strands of the humble life: dealing with mistreatment, having a certain degree of compassion for those who are badly off, responding to those who are flourishing, respecting the independence of others without being inadequately concerned, taking one's own independence with the proper seriousness, living lavishly or more simply. I then offer a few further points to complete the picture of what it is to be humble.

IS
HUMILITY
A
VIRTUE?

To be humble, says the *Oxford English Dictionary*, is to have "a low estimate of oneself." Evidently, that conception was standard in the late nineteenth century as well, as Henry Sidgwick reports in *Methods of Ethics*: "For it is generally said that humility prescribes a low opinion of our merits."[1] But if humility is low self-esteem, where does this leave the rather splendid among us, those in whom such a view of oneself would seem to display quite astonishing ignorance, if not extensive self-deception?

One answer is that actually there are no splendid human beings. No matter who you are, according to Bernard of Clairvaux, "if you examine yourself inwardly by the light of truth and without dissimulation, and judge yourself without flattery; no doubt you will be humbled in your own eyes, becoming contemptible in your own sight as a result of this true knowledge of yourself."[2]

Fortunately, Bernard's depressing view is not obviously correct. In fact, it is difficult to see a reason to hold such a view, apart from the sort that would have satisfied Martin Luther, for example. Luther believed that we are all so corrupted by Adam's original sin as to be beyond redemption by any apparent virtues.[3] Assuming one does not share that belief, however, the problem remains: if to be humble is to have a low opinion of oneself, there do appear to be people who could be humble only through self-deception or ignorance.

That is troubling, because why humility of such a sort should be admirable is not at all clear. Never to appreciate one's good qualities might conceivably be endearing, like a tendency to get flustered easily, but for it to be morally estimable is something else again. Here is Sidgwick on the subject:

> It would seem just as irrational to underrate ourselves as to overrate. . . . I think that if we reflect carefully on the common judgments in which the notion of Humility is used, we shall find that the quality commonly *praised* under this name . . . is not properly regulative of the opinions we form of ourselves—for here as in other opinions we ought to aim at nothing but Truth.[4]

Such a view is not properly regulative, some might say, because extensive false beliefs about oneself are bound to bring trouble in the long run. It is not properly regulative, others might say, because to live under a misconception, however happily or unhappily, is simply wrong.

Could we perhaps avoid the problem, not by denying that anyone is meritorious, but by denying that the meritorious are capable of genuine humility? According to Gabriele Taylor, for example, "The man who accepts his lowly position as what is due him is the man who has humility, or the humble man."[5] This precludes humility in anyone who has a high position (earned through hard work, for example). Even if such a person were quite diffident about his achievement, his diffidence would not count: he would have to leave his humility behind, along with his humble origins.

Such a restriction is especially unappealing, however, in that normally we not only allow that those who rise can be humble but we find them especially admirable when they are. "To have done all that and still retained his humility," we might marvel, clearly meaning, not that something logically impossible had been carried off, but that something especially remarkable had been.

In short, there do seem to be praiseworthy people in the world, and this is awkward, if to be humble is to have a low opinion of oneself. For, such people are logically capable of humility and perhaps even especially praiseworthy for their humility. But, in them, humility would be erroneous, a matter either of ignorance or of self-deception. It is hard to see how such a thing could be a virtue at all, let alone an especially admirable one.

In addition, suppose that someone did have a low opinion of herself, and that this was quite justified: her bad points did far outweigh her good, just as she thought. This attitude might permeate her life, making none of her deeds or (few) virtues a matter of any pride for her. But, it seems, this attitude also might not permeate her life. She might consider herself a loser overall while positively preening over something more specific. Indeed, she might be quite obnoxious about this more specific matter, taking it far more seriously than it deserved, making it part of every conversation, insisting on our deference in this one particular. With all this, calling her humble would be awkward, despite her having suitably low (global) self-esteem. And yet, if, instead, being humble means taking a persistently dim view of every particular in one's behavior and character, it is hard to imagine anything more dreary. How could this be a virtue, something one might hope to make part of one's personality?

There are problems with seeing humility as a virtue, if humility consists in having a low opinion of oneself. Some of the difficulties arise when a low opinion of oneself would be mistaken; others arise when it would not be. So, whether humility should be pictured in a different way altogether is worth considering.

<h1 style="text-align: center;">1</h1>

Occasionally someone strikes us as a person of great dignity. Why? What gives this impression? After remarking, "No two of us might answer this question in exactly the same way," Aurel Kolnai offers the following: "First—the qualities of composure, calmness, restraint, reserve. . . . Secondly—the qualities of distinctness, delimitation, and distance; of something . . . intangible, invulnerable, inaccessible to destructive or corruptive or subversive interference. . . . Thirdly . . . of self-controlled serenity. . . . With its firm stance and solid immovability, the dignified defies the world."[6] Dignified people have these qualities, not because they are unconscious of "destructive or corruptive or subversive" influences, but because they are not vulnerable to these influences. Thus, the dignified judge is not unaware of the obnoxious defendant but simply presides beyond the fellow's reach. The judge cannot be baited into departing from a certain range of behavior—let alone is he likely to send his robes flying in an Irish jig for the sheer fun of it. His solemn demeanor represents a firm sense of who he is and how he (therefore) should act, a sense not easily undermined.

Similarly, consider those whose dignity is especially striking because they retain their dignity under what might easily be humiliating circumstances. There is the garbageman whose way of carrying himself shows he does not think *himself* garbage, or the woman in service who is nobody's servant, or the elderly lady now sunk into genteel poverty. They all consider themselves persons of quality who should behave in certain ways and who should be treated with a proper respect by others. They resist pressures to think less of themselves and to act the parts of these lesser persons. Finally, notice that the pressures are spurious: these people have a proper sense of their worth and their roles, not a misconception.

In sum, to have dignity is to appreciate oneself sufficiently that one would withstand spurious pressures to lower one's self-esteem. Lest the phrasing make this sound too intellectualized, let me emphasize that these self-images are expressed in behavior: in the dignified garbageman's personal tidiness, the maid's proud bearing, the impoverished gentlewoman's careful toilette, the judge's solemnity. Their circumstances might seem to call for them to live differently; their dignity consists in their having too firm a grasp of who they are to heed that call.

Humility should be understood similarly, I want to suggest. Humility too involves having an accurate sense of oneself, sufficiently firm to resist pressures toward incorrect revisions. Only, here the pressures are to think too much of oneself, rather than too little.

The standard temptations would be accomplishments and praise. You have just returned from scaling a difficult mountain, and we are suitably impressed, for your feat required great skill and stellar qualities of character. To think of oneself as so endowed and to have the attention and praise that such an achievement merits can be gratifying indeed. We would understand your wanting these things to continue, your wanting to remain the center of attention a bit longer than the accomplishment merits: your wanting it to have been even more of a feat than it was.

Morcover, it is possible not merely to *want* more of this than you deserve but to think it your *due*. Since more is not your due, here your sense of your own worth has become skewed. You have come to think too highly of yourself, just as the garbageman might have come to think too little of himself. You have yielded to a temptation to cast yourself in a more central role, where the spotlight ought to linger and the player is entitled to dominate the action. The recasting is behavioral.

Perhaps you demand that our conversation not turn to other topics; perhaps you believe yourself entitled to your host's wife. Each would be failure of humility, I want to say, in that each is a failure to resist temptations to overestimate oneself and one's accomplishments.

For a different illustration, consider the following. It depicts boastfulness in a twelfth-century monk, but it might apply quite comfortably to an academic or two of your acquaintance.

> He must either talk or burst. . . . He interrupts a questioner, he answers one who does not ask. He himself puts the questions, he himself solves them, he cuts short his fellow speaker's unfinished words. . . . He does not care to teach you, or to learn from you what he does not know, but to know that you know that he knows.[7]

This is boastful, I want to say, insofar as the monk is overestimating his own talents relative to those of others. To be humble, I suggest, is to understand oneself sufficiently clearly to resist temptations to such behavior.

Now for a complication: there is more than one standard by which to estimate, and what is satisfying when judged by one of these may seem paltry, at best, when judged by another. What then is it to overestimate—or, in humility, to resist overestimation? Suppose, for example, that you have just had an article accepted by a leading journal. You have never been successful there before. In fact, this is much better than you ever did earlier in your career, and as you think of your progress, you are pleased. There are other ways to look at things, though. How does your work compare to what your colleagues are doing? To the work of contemporaries at similar institutions? To that of the leading philosophers of the day? To the Nichomachean Ethics, or the Theory of Descriptions?

Some of these comparisons will be deflating—"humbling," as we sometimes say. What then is a proper humility about your accomplishment? What would it be to keep the thing in perspective? On one view, since what you have done is nothing much when compared to something truly magnificent, to keep your accomplishment in perspective would be to treat it as if it *were* nothing. You should take no pride in your accomplishment at all but treat it as trivial, even be a little embarrassed at any inclination to be proud of it. Perhaps something like this underlies the thinking about humility of Saint Paul, Saint Augustine, and Martin Luther: that is, because God and his works are so magnificent, whatever you are or have done is trivial by comparison, and your human pride in who you are or what you have done is laughable.[8]

I want to suggest instead that proper humility requires, not that you take no pride at all in what you have done, but only that you be no more proud than your accomplishment merits. Thus, the failure would be in treating what is only a fairly nice piece of writing as if it called for a *Festschrift*, or for mention in future histories of philosophy. The piece is not *that* good, and so you would be overestimating it, and yourself, if you were to act as if it were. But to say that you overestimate your writing if you take any pride in it at all entails that only the truly magnificent is cause for *any* pride. I do not believe there is a compelling reason to hold that, and I believe it is false.

Indeed an unwillingness to judge oneself by any but the very highest standards can reflect, not humility, but its opposite. For, such unwillingness can embody a conviction that one belongs in a higher league, so to speak, that achievement by local standards is insignificant because one's talents call for a higher standard of judgment. Insofar as judging oneself by the highest standards overestimates those talents, it is a failure of humility, rather than an expression of it.

2

Despite the examples, the analysis might seem incomplete, in that it does not specify which people or forms of behavior are humble. It does connect humility with resistance to over-estimation, but it does not say when one would be over-estimating. Actually, this is not a fault in the analysis but a respect in which it resembles observing that selfishness consists in taking more than one's fair share. That is what selfishness is, even though (since it does not specify what a fair share would be), it does not specify which actions are selfish.

In the same way, the analysis of humility will not by itself specify whether, for example, it is a failure of humility for me to think I can write something interesting about a certain philosophical topic. That would depend on whether in making the attempt I would exaggerate my abilities. However, this in turn depends both on what my abilities are and on what the proper credentials for the attempt would be. So, the matter is not settled by the fact that humility consists in understanding oneself too clearly to be readily moved to exaggeration. To settle it, we would need more than an analysis of humility.

For a full picture of which actions are humble, we would need a full theory of human worth, such as Bernard of Clairvaux's theory that all of us are contemptible and thus that *any* self-assertion is overreaching. I do not share that view; nor do I share the view that no human virtue or accomplishment should bring any satisfaction because none is comparable to God's. I have no rival theory to offer. My point is that any such theory goes beyond the *analysis* of humility, the matter about which I do want to offer a view.

Specifically, I have suggested that there are difficulties with analyzing humility as having a low opinion of oneself, and that we should think of it instead as an inclination to keep one's accomplishments, traits, and so on in unexaggerated perspective, even if stimulated to exaggerate.

Against this might be the objection that, although keeping one's accomplishments and virtues in perspective is commendable, it is not humility, exactly, because it permits a *somewhat* rosy view of oneself and some enjoyment of attention. Whereas, the objection would run, in our experience the truly humble do not consider themselves at all remarkable and are positively embarrassed by praise and attention. "It wasn't anything," the humble hero will say; "anybody would have done it," even though it is obvious to us that *we* would not have. The humble hero, it seems, does not merely limit himself to the attention he deserves and resist natural temptations to bask: he would prefer not to have even what he does deserve.

One way to read this objection is that only the behavior described qualifies as humble. On this version, if the hero were embarrassed only by excessive attention and enjoyed whatever attention he actually deserved, he would not count as humble. This statement is too strong, surely. Some of the humble may be as shy of attention as this, but it is hard to see such shyness as a *sine qua non*.

Still, there appear to be problems for my analysis if we allow even that *some* of the humble are as described. For, I have identified humility with having a proper sense of oneself and one's accomplishments. The hero's behavior does not show this proper sense but shows an improper one. He *under*values himself, takes his deed to call not for the spotlight but for the farthest shadows. So, it seems, his behavior cannot express humility, on my analysis, not even one species of humility.

Notice, however, that shunning the praise and attention one deserves need not betray an improper sense of oneself or of what one has done. It is possible simply not to *want* these things, while fully recognizing that one deserves them. A person can prefer a different form of acknowledgment, not because this is the essence of humility, but because of other traits: shyness, for example, or dislike of even the appearance of arrogance. So, tho hero's shying from praise is certainly consistent with his being humble, in the sense of understanding what he deserves.

Still, the objection was, not that the hero could not be a humble person, on my view, but that his shunning the attention he deserved could not *express* that humility. How could rejecting something one deserved express a proper sense of oneself and one's accomplishment? The objection was that the (deeply humble) hero cannot be acting humbly, on my analysis, since his behavior cannot express this proper sense of things. Yet, he does seem to be one of our paradigms of humility as he backs away from the plaudits he richly deserves.

The way to preserve this intuition is not to abandon the analysis, however. That would return us to the problematic equation of humility with underestimation. Suppose we acknowledge instead that, very often, it might be the hero who is right to think our reaction excessive, rather than we who are right to think him too modest. Perhaps he knows better than we how hard or how easy the deed was for him, or what his motivation was, or how clearly he understood what he was doing. (He need not be particularly articulate about these things to be in that position—he knows by having been the one who did it.) Thus perhaps when humble heroes reject our spotlight it is not because they undervalue themselves and what they did but precisely because their grasp of these things is too firm for them to join our overevaluation—precisely because they are humble, that is. Those who truly are underestimating themselves are not expressing humility, on my view, but those who simply reject attention certainly can be.

Finally, what about a person of an opposite kind: someone who (far from shrinking from our praise) strides happily forward in anticipation of it; someone whose great accomplishments have made him entirely full of himself? Surely *he* ought not to count as humble. And yet, if he is entitled to put on those airs, given the wonderful things he has done, then he is not exaggerating his importance when he does so and he is suitably humble after all, on the account I have offered. Certainly this must be a flaw in the account?

The reply to this objection is that anyone who truly was full of himself and putting on airs would be exaggerating, since no accomplishment calls for one to do that. Indeed, those are precisely the expressions we use to describe people who go too far—people who are not humble, on my account, just as the objector urges that they are not. Of course, we do sometimes misdescribe with these phrases, out of envy or simple failure to appreciate the other person's accomplishment. Our using them does not guarantee their accuracy, any more than our inclination to gush over heroism guarantees that we are not exaggerating. The other party might be right to be as proud as he is, just as he might be right to be less impressed than we are.

3

What about the questions with which we began: can a truly accomplished person be humble, and, if so, why should humility be especially admirable in such a person? There is no problem with the first of these on the suggested analysis, it turns out: even great success certainly does not preclude one's being a person whose head would not be turned by success. Nor does the lack of great success. So, there is no opposite problem about how a person whose life was largely a failure could be humble.

It is also clear enough how humility might be a virtue, on this construal, since it will not involve ignorance of one's merits or self-deception about them. As Sidgwick says, we should aim at true opinion in all things, including our understanding of ourselves. To be humble is to be resistant to a particularly tempting sort of error in this matter. Such resistance might be especially admirable in the accomplished because they will have withstood many such temptations. By the same token, it would also be especially admirable in those for whom the trials are fewer but especially severe: those whose first accomplishments are very highly praised, for example, and those whose success comes while they are quite young, and so on.

Notice too that much of the exaggerated praise such people receive and manage to resist is perfectly sincere. It expresses the honest opinion and admiration of those who offer it. Hence, to remain unswayed by exaggerated praise is not simply a matter of being able to spot flatterers and those with ulterior motives. Just to be able to tell when people are lying to you for purposes of their own is not enough: you must also be able to tell when they are simply wrong. Making that distinction requires a clear sense of the achievement in question, of what exactly happened on the occasion for which you are being praised, and what it means about you. This is a very different kind of perceptiveness from the ability to tell when people do not mean what they say to you.

In short, when a truly accomplished person is unpersuaded by exaggerated praise and retains his humility, here is what is happening. First, he is being offered an account of himself that would be very gratifying to accept. Second, this account is offered him not only by flatterers but by people who sincerely believe it to be true. They urge him to accept this highly desirable thing as his due. For him to hang on to reality under such conditions seems to require a combination of honesty and clarity of vision that is truly remarkable. No wonder we are so impressed by such people.

Not that we do not have some initial doubts about them, some skepticism that they can really be as they seem. We are not sure anyone could be quite this strong, perhaps because we doubt we would be ourselves. At any rate, our doubts are plausible enough, not cheaply cynical, but reasonably realistic about human nature.

Notice, though, that the idea of a highly accomplished person being humble is certainly not a ridiculous one, on this analysis. It was ridiculous on the earlier analysis, where this would consist in taking a dim view of what is obviously admirable. For, how could this superior person fail to see what is so plain to the rest of us? That would be hard to believe, not because it is hard to believe anyone could be so good and so strong, but because it is hard to believe anyone could be so blind: especially, anyone so otherwise impressive. To believe that his humility was a pretense would be more plausible by far.

Thus, by rethinking humility in the way suggested, we redeem the possibility that the humility of those who have much of which to be proud is not always *false* humility. That is a point in favor of rethinking it. Indeed, there is much more to say about this new conception of humility, and the rest of this book explores it. However, false humility is an intriguing phenomenon in its own right, well worth a brief discussion before we go on.

When we suspect someone of false humility, often it is because he has "laid it on too thick": he has declined our praise so strenuously and understated his achievement so greatly that we doubt we are hearing his true views. We suspect his true views are much more admiring than the ones to which he is pretending.

Now, since his performance is meant to convince us that he is humble, he is likely to play to what he sees as our conception of humility. He is likely to act as he thinks his audience would expect a humble person to act. As we have seen, in many quarters that would mean acting as if he thought very little of his accomplishment, as if he were astonished we should be impressed, and so on. Accordingly, his act will be a difficult one to carry off, since, as mentioned, this is also the very sort of thing it will be hard for the audience to credit. People who have this audience's conception of humility rightly suspect that most humility is false: that is, that most people do not really undervalue what they have done. Most people do not; so, most who act as if they did are frauds and should not be believed.

Notice too that our man's performance does not portray the attitude that a genuinely humble person would take, if the arguments here have been sound. For, a genuinely humble person would not have so low an opinion of himself as our man is pretending to have. Thus, this typical variety of false humility does not consist in (falsely) acting as a humble person would. It consists in acting as such a person's audience would (wrongly) expect such a person to act, so as to be thought humble by them: here, by overplaying matters in a way that (ironically) is also likely to arouse suspicion.

Imagine next an audience that does not misunderstand humility in this way. This group does not picture it as underestimating oneself, that is, but (roughly) as having oneself in unexaggerated perspective. Now imagine someone who wishes to convince these people that she is humble, even though she is not. What will *her* false humility be like?

Once again, her aim is to convince the audience of something that is not true. She knows that actually she is not humble, that is, that actually she thinks more highly of herself than she should. Her plan is to pretend to a more modest opinion. More precisely, her plan is to pretend to the view her audience would consider an accurate one. For her to discern what that would be may be difficult, since it is not a view she shares and finds natural. So, she may go overboard, pretending to an even lower opinion than this; she too may lay it on too thick, that is, and risk detection.

Alternatively, she might strike just the right note. She might even manage to behave in just the way a humble person would. Then her chief worry will be that this might be so unusual for her that the audience will see through it even so. Regardless of whether they do see through her, however, her humility will have been only an act rather than a representation of her true attitude. Her performance will differ considerably from that of the pretenders who overdo, but it will still be a performance, and her humility will still be false humility.

All these varieties of false humility are duplicitous. Sometimes, the duplicity is repellent; sometimes, it is pathetic. Either way, false humility is not something we are likely to find morally appealing, unlike the real thing. Genuine humility is perfectly free of pretense, and a number of reasons have been offered for admiring it. Bernard of Clairvaux once made an additional claim on its behalf that seems even more plausible if we replace his conception of humility with the one proposed here. Bernard advises as follows:

> Observe what you are, that you are wretched indeed, and so learn to be merciful, a thing you cannot know in any other way. For if you regard your neighbor's faults but do not observe your own, you are likely to be moved not to ruth but to wrath, not to condole but to condemn, not to restore in the spirit of meekness but to destroy in the spirit of anger.[9]

By being merciful, Bernard meant reacting in a tolerant, sympathetic way to behavior that was faulty and would ordinarily make one resentful and inclined to retaliate. Only the humble will react in this tolerant way, says he. Only they will think, not "That so-and-so," but "I might have done the same"; only they will think: "He's only human—none of us is perfect."

Now, it does seem plausible that someone who thought himself faultless would not be capable of being understanding in this way, and that the more thoroughly you knew your own shortcomings the more understanding you could be. More precisely, although the contempt for oneself that Bernard prescribes does not seem to be a necessary precondition, some more limited degree of humility does. There is a further question, though: is it really a good thing about humility that it conduces to regarding mistreatment in this tolerant, sympathetic way?

Not everyone would think so. For some, any failure to take offense is a failure to respect oneself properly. According to Jeffrie Murphy, for example, "If I count morally as much as anyone else (as surely I do), a failure to resent moral injuries done to me is a failure to care about the moral value incarnate in my own personality (that I am, in Kantian language, an end-in-myself)."[10]

The next chapter explores this matter more thoroughly. For now it might suffice to suggest that universal tolerance of the kind Bernard apparently favored *is* morally dubious, just as Murphy would say, but that more limited generosity toward those who wrong us is not only respectable but positively admirable. Certainly a person can take herself too lightly, and accepting mistreatment as her due exemplifies this. But, it is not obvious that *every* misdeed demands resentment, however trivial and however oft performed by oneself. There is such a thing as recognizing that the other person is (merely) human, like oneself, and therefore bound to err in minor, perhaps familiar, ways. That reaction is not identical with servility, since it does not accept any suggestion that one does not "count morally as much as anyone else." So, it really ought not to trouble Murphy.

Fortunately, all that seems likely to result from acquaintance with one's own flaws is a limited generosity of spirit. The contrary inclination to strike back, especially against those who seriously mistreat us, is surely among our strongest inclinations, perhaps for reasons rooted in evolution. So, the (limited) workings of humility in this regard do seem to recommend it.

There is, of course, a broader concern that to be humble is to lack self-respect. The Bible equates humility with meekness, after all, and meekness is central to the "slave morality" Nietzsche so despised. An image arises of someone who not only accepts mistreatment but also shrinks from putting himself forward when he should: someone in need of what we now call assertiveness training. How could *that* be a desirable trait of character?

On one hand, this concern is perfectly appropriate, it seems to me, if to be humble is to have contempt for oneself, because self-contempt seems to call for this accepting and shrinking behavior. Perhaps even having a low estimate of oneself also calls for this kind of behavior. On the other hand, if, as I have suggested, humility consists in taking oneself neither more nor less seriously than one should, it would not call for anything like this. For, there is no good reason to think that contempt is proper self-regard, or that one's self-esteem would have to be low if it were accurate. Humility thus coexists with appropriately positive feelings about oneself, feelings founded not in error—as with the improperly proud—but in self-knowledge

Perhaps this establishes, at most, that it is not a bad thing to be humble in the way I have construed humility, as it might be a bad thing to be contemptuous of oneself. As to why humility is a positively good thing, we have so far the suggestions that it combines honesty and clarity of moral vision, and that it conduces to a virtuous spirit of forgiveness. There are at least two further points in its favor.

First, for the most part a person who is a good judge of his or her own achievements and virtues should also be a good judge of others, at least in the same particulars. That is, the ability to resist overestimating the relative importance of having won the race or published the article should insure a similar accuracy of judgment when the accomplishment is another person's. After all, it is the same thing being judged, this time without the psychological pressure to overvalue it.

There may also be less pressure to undervalue the deeds of others as well, if one is humble: less inclination to protect one's self-image by discounting what they have done, because one's self-image is not inflated. If I think I am an incredible human being, it is hard to agree that you are one as well: the point of exaggerating one's value seems to be to stand out from others. By contrast, an accurate self-image needs no such protection from reality. So if there is a connection between the ability to maintain a realistic assessment of one's own accomplishments, abilities, and virtues and a similar accuracy in one's understanding of others, then humility is part of broad good judgment. That is something of obvious value.

Second, is there not also a connection between understanding oneself and having reasonable expectations of oneself? If I understand myself, I know better than to think I am the one to fix the car or to argue our case before the zoning board. That is a good thing for all of us, including me, since it means I defer to the more able or, in their absence, understand both how serious my effort has to be and how limited my chances are, and have a patience with my bumbling efforts that I would not have if I expected the task to yield more readily. We have a better chance to succeed, and if we do fail through my efforts, the disappointment should be more manageable.

An inclination to forgive, good judgment of others, and reasonable expectations of oneself: perhaps these advantages do not make humility the supreme virtue, but they do seem to call for putting it on the list. If so, unlike self-contempt and low self-regard, humility is a virtue that could be present without paradox in a person who deserved high regard.

Suppose you were a humble person; what effect would this have on the way you lived your life? Thus far, we have only certain broad indications. In later chapters we explore what more can be worked out. First, however, I want to describe a different posture toward the project, according to which it will not be humility we will be exploring but something else. On this other view, humility does consist in having a very low opinion of oneself, just as Bernard of Clairvaux thought it did. Admittedly, for a person to retain such an opinion when those around him are singing his praises is difficult. This can be managed, though, by keeping in mind that no earthly accomplishment is of any importance at all: not one's own, not Edmund Hillary's, not Einstein's—not anyone's. In this way, it is possible for the "accomplished" person to be humble—to think badly of himself, that is—just as we believe it is. And, for him to do so is the remarkable achievement we take it to be.

Is humility also a virtue in such a person, on this view? Is it a virtue in anyone, for that matter? Actually these are not proper questions to ask, on the view I am describing. What we can do is to observe that humility is *regarded as* a virtue by those who belong to certain traditions. Specifically, humility is admired by those who belong to the Christian tradition, as it is broadly called. If you are a Christian yourself, you have a reason to value humility too, as part of the larger package; if you are not, it is harder to see why you should. You might be tempted to value it, as a vestige of early days in Sunday School and faint memories of verses about "gentle Jesus, meek and mild". But perhaps you should resist this temptation, given that you do not accept the broader picture in which admiring humility has its comfortable place.

I do not take this approach to the topic, myself, for several reasons. A major one is that, as this other approach has things, when Bernard of Clairvaux and his ilk admired humility, they were admiring low self-esteem. But why say this? Why not say that they admired a person's retaining what they considered to be an *accurate* conception of himself, especially in the face of temptations to value earthly achievements and human praise more highly than they thought such things should be valued? Why think of Bernard and the others as impressed by thinking badly of oneself as such, that is? What would that ever have had to be said for it?

Nothing at all, so far as I can see. So this view makes the early Christian thinkers mysteriously perverse in their admiration of humility. It is a little like imagining a people who

value nasty sensations, not because they think these are deserved punishment or a test of courage or some such thing, but
for the unpleasant way the sensations feel to them. It puts
such people beyond our ken, and any view that makes other
human beings this alien should be regarded with suspicion.

It seems much more plausible to take it that Bernard and
the others valued understanding oneself aright and just differed from us about what such understanding would reveal.
They differed from us over that because they held certain
well-known views about God and about man's fall from grace,
from which their conclusions follow plausibly enough. They
valued the same thing we might value—roughly, resistance to
overvaluing oneself—and credited it to those we consider to
have been too hard on themselves.

Accordingly, I take it to be humility we are exploring
when we think about what it is to understand oneself aright.

2

MISTREATMENT

Suppose we flatter someone rather outrageously, and she gives every indication of thinking that we are simply speaking the truth. This gives us good reason to doubt her humility. The only question is whether her agreement with our inflated remarks is genuine.

A person's response to mistreatment can be equally revealing. It is possible to overreact to mistreatment, that is, in a way that shows pretty clearly that you have an inflated picture of yourself. You can take the episode to have been a far more major event in the history of the universe than it was, something calling for abject apology from the wrongdoer and extensive sympathy from outsiders. Typically, to act as if wronging you is an especially big deal is to act as if you were a big deal yourself. Typically, that is, overreacting to mistreatment displays a lack of humility as readily as agreeing with flattery.

This is tricky, though, since it is possible not only to overreact when mistreated but also to underreact. Accepting abuse as no worse than you deserve shows a lack of self-respect. So you can take yourself too lightly as well as too seriously. What would it be to react just as you should to whatever mistreatment came your way, so that you erred in neither direction?

That is a question of special interest, for two reasons. First, mistreatment is part of everyone's life. Even the most fortunate of us experience it, albeit only in its more minor forms. Some people seem to pay this part of their lives intense attention. Others are more "philosophical" about it. Here is a chance to see how humility would incline a person in this universal aspect of life.

Second, the reaction to mistreatment that humility ordains may be the one respect in which humility seems most indistinguishable from a lack of proper self-respect. If humility really does call for meek acceptance of whatever others do to us, how does it differ from taking ourselves too lightly? And if it does not call for that but for something more self-respecting, what does it call for? Here is a chance to consider the matter closely.

I start with initial reactions to being mistreated: with taking offense in the first place, that is. One question is what self-respect does demand, along these lines; another, what humility demands. The answers to these questions make plain whether the two pull in opposite directions. Later, I take up the question of extending forgiveness to those who did one wrong, to see how humility would incline a person in this regard.

1

One view is that we ought never to take offense at any mistreatment we suffer, and that we should forgive all those whom we take to have wronged us. This might be held on a number of different grounds, some of which do not connect it with being properly humble. For example, resentment is sometimes viewed as bad for the person who harbors it, so that we should all strive to overcome it: not in order to be suitably humble, exactly, but just as good mental hygiene. Similarly, it is sometimes argued that God will forgive us our own misdeeds only insofar as we have practiced forgiveness ourselves. Here again it appears not to be humility that counsels forgiveness but a dubious kind of prudence. Since these arguments do not have to do with humility, they are outside our present concern.[1]

More relevant is a view of human nature that has proven congenial to religious writers as seemingly diverse as Bernard of Clairvaux and Jonathan Edwards. On this view, each of us is so worthless that whatever "mistreatment" befalls us is never any worse than we deserve. Accordingly, to take offense is always to overestimate oneself, and to refuse to forgive is to continue in this presumptuous posture. In other words, humility does call for us to accept mistreatment without complaint, rather than acting as if we deserved anything better.

Here I want to consider a very different conception of human nature, however, put forward (among other places) by Jeffrie Murphy in the writings cited earlier. On this other conception, we each have various rights, and the violation of those rights ought to arouse our resentment. If we fail to resent the violation of our rights, we express not a humility suited to our worthlessness but a disgraceful lack of self-respect. As Murphy puts it:

> I am, in short, suggesting that the primary value defended by the passion of resentment is *self-respect*, that proper self-respect is essentially tied to the passion of resentment, and that a person who does not resent moral injuries done to him . . . is almost necessarily a person lacking in self-respect.[2]

Nor should the victim seek too readily to overcome this resentful reaction and extend forgiveness.

> If I am correct in linking resentment to self-respect, a too ready tendency to forgive may properly be re-

garded as a *vice* because it may be a sign that one lacks respect for oneself.[3]

The main rationale Murphy offers for this line of thought is that to be wronged is to be insulted, and that we ought to resent insults.

> One reason we so deeply resent moral injuries done to us is not simply that they hurt us in some tangible or sensible way; it is because such injuries are also *messages*—symbolic communications. They are ways a wrongdoer has of saying to us, "I count but you do not." . . . Intentional wrongdoing *insults* us and attempts (sometimes successfully) to degrade us.[4]

This line of reasoning recurs:

> Wrongdoers attempt (sometimes successfully) to degrade or insult us; to bring us low; to say "I am on high while you are down there below." As a result, we in a real sense *lose face* when done a moral injury—one reason why easy forgiveness tends to compromise self-esteem.[5]

The idea is that a self-respecting person will not simply accept an insult as if it were true, but will resent having been insulted. She might later forgive the person who insulted her, but for this to be consistent with her self-respect something will have to be done about the insult. For example, the wrongdoer could repent.

> Then the insulting message is no longer present— no longer endorsed by the wrongdoer. . . . Of such a person it cannot be said that he is *now* conveying

the message that he holds me in contempt. Thus I
can relate to him now, through forgiveness, without
fearing my own acquiescence in immorality or in
judgments that I lack worth.[6]

Where the insult stands unabated, though, the resentment
should stand as well.

This reasoning starts from a contention that we each
have a basic worth, which we should respect and should insist that others respect. Predictably, this reasoning reaches a
very different conclusion than is reached by those whose starting point is that we are worthless. It counsels resentment and
is dubious of acceptance, where the other tradition counsels
acceptance and abhors resentment.

There are examples of mistreatment that fit Murphy's
line very appealingly. Think of the husband who shames his
wife by conducting his adulteries in public, bringing his various women to company functions and virtually inhaling them
on the spot. This is as much as to say, "My wife just has to
accept this. She would never make it on her own, and she
would never find anyone who would treat her with more respect." It surely seems right to think that she would resent
such treatment, if she had any self-respect.

In *The Sun Also Rises*, Ernest Hemingway provides another character congenial to Murphy's thesis in the beautiful
Lady Brett. Brett simply does whatever pleases her, with no
regard for the cost to others. It is not that she bears them malice, for they are not that much in her thoughts. She is simply
indifferent to others, except as sources of enjoyment.

That indifference proves unbearable to one of its chief
victims, despite his remarkable willingness to accept treatment that is more directly insulting. He takes it more or less in
stride when he is ridiculed to someone he later describes as
his only friend, again when he is told in so many words that
he is "not wanted" and should go away so that others can

have a good time, again when he is told that he "amounts to nothing," and when he is publicly compared to a steer (remember, this is Hemingway).[8] In each case, part of the point is to hurt him, but he is not much affected. What he eventually cannot bear, however, is Lady Brett's utter indifference to him.

> I just couldn't stand it about Brett. I've been through hell, Jake. It's been simply hell. When I met her down here Brett treated me as though I were a perfect stranger. I just couldn't stand it. We lived together at San Sebastian. I suppose you know it. I can't stand it anymore.[9]

Let us suppose that Lady Brett's victim deserves better treatment than she gives him, so that she does him wrong by being so indifferent. We might also plausibly say, with Murphy, that Lady Brett's behavior insults him: it suggests that he deserves no more consideration than a lamppost and, perhaps, that he has been a fool to think there was something special between them.

So there clearly is mistreatment that is insulting. But Murphy's contention is universal: he takes us to be insulted *whenever* we are done wrong, and this is not so clear. Consider for a moment mistreatment that is oddly flattering: the competitor who cheats because he thinks you would win if the competition were fair, or the artist who forges another's work. These wrongdoers do not seem to "hold . . . in contempt" the people they wrong, to use Murphy's phrase, in at all the same way as the flagrant adulterer does his wife or Lady Brett her former lover. Similarly, it does not seem that there is contempt and an attempt to degrade when a wrongdoer genuinely believes that she is not mistreating you, if she has some good reasons for her point of view. Suppose she is wrong; even so, since the two of you simply have a reasonable disagreement over whether you are being mistreated, it does not seem as if self-respect demands you take offense and demand satisfaction. In short, it does not seem as if all mistreatment is humiliating and, therefore, requires us to respond as if we had been humiliated.

Murphy's answer to all this would run as follows, I think. By definition, to wrong you is to treat you less well than you deserve to be treated. By definition, the wrongdoer has not given you and your interests the weight they should have but has (wrongly) weighted something else more heavily. He has demoted you, in effect. Murphy puts it this way: "A failure to resent moral injuries done to me is a failure to care about the moral value incarnate in my own person (that I am, in Kantian language, an end in myself) and thus a failure to care about the very rules of morality."[10]

Notice, though, that there is nothing personal in this sort of demotion. The behavior expresses no derision toward anyone as an individual. If there is an insult here, it is to something you share with everyone, a kind of moral status that everyone has and that is expressed (very abstractly) in the moral rules the wrongdoer violates. The question is, if we are self-respecting must we take offense at these impersonal insults, on behalf of our Kantian souls? So that not to do so will be a failure of self-respect, as well as a failure to have the proper respect for morality itself? I want to suggest that we need not.

To see why not, imagine first someone who takes no offense because she simply holds a false moral view. To her way of thinking, it was not wrong for you to treat her as you did, because it would not be wrong for anyone to treat anyone in this way. It is not that she has no conception of right and wrong, nor that she thinks human beings are so worthless that it is impossible to act wrongly toward them. She is simply mistaken about some of the rules of morality—not unlike the rest of us, no doubt. Because of this mistake, she sometimes does not take offense when she has been wronged.

On Murphy's view, she shows a lack of self-respect on those occasions by failing to accord herself that high status that the moral rules express. Presumably she also fails to respect others as she should when she is equally sanguine about their suffering this same treatment. Now, why should we say these things? It cannot be that self-respect requires getting one's moral status *right*: then there would be a lack of self-respect in overestimating one's moral status, which is a very odd idea indeed. It must be that what self-respect requires is that one not peg oneself too low.

Does our woman do that, though? Remember that she pegs herself no lower than she does anyone else. Does she then peg all of us too low? Well, she thinks we do not have a right that in fact we do have, and this does seem to demote us in a way. But she also thinks we have a right that we *do not* have—the right to act in the way in question—and that seems to elevate us in the same way. Evidently, what she has is just a different conception of our moral status, not necessarily a reductive one. And, surely, to conceive of us differently is not necessarily to accord us too little respect.

In short, a person who takes no offense when mistreated may be expressing a false moral view, rather than a lack of self-respect, if she regards the behavior with the same equanimity when she is not its victim. Her failure to care about the rules of morality is not a failure to care about herself. A lack of self-respect seems instead to be displayed most clearly, not when someone fails to take certain misbehavior to be wrong, but when she takes it to be wrong except when it is done to her.

For example, suppose that Charles has failed to meet you as he promised, not for any good reason, but just because something more interesting came up. Suppose that you would never do such a thing yourself, and that you are distressed when others are treated this way. We might well expect you to be angry on your own behalf as well—but you are not. You do not take yourself to deserve the same consideration as others; you wrongly put yourself beneath them. In short: you lack self-respect.

There are variations. In this first little story, you take only yourself too lightly, and your reasons for doing so are not indicated. It is also possible to lack self-respect in a different way; for example, as part of a mistaken broader feeling of racial inferiority. There, you wrongly consider it acceptable to treat not just yourself but any person of your race in a way you consider it wrong to treat people of another race.

Feeling that you are second class because you are "only a woman" or an immigrant or somebody from the shop floor is similar. In each of these, there is a reason why you do not respect yourself (or anyone who shares what you take to be your stigma). Each is nevertheless a case of lacking self-respect because, in each, you wrongly demote yourself from a class you take to have certain rights. You fail to universalize, to use philosophers' language; only, unlike the usual illustrations of that, you fail not by elevating yourself above others but by placing yourself beneath them.

Humility does not require us to engage in such behavior, however. Indeed, having a reasonably clear grasp of who you are should have exactly the opposite effect: you would know better than to think you belong in a lower class. So, if a lack of self-respect is nothing more than an inclination to demote oneself, we are certainly wrong to connect it with having humility.

This might seem a bit too quick, though. It might be objected that there is another way of lacking self-respect, which these arguments do not reach. The arguments require only that we be consistent, that we respect ourselves no less than we respect comparable others. The objection would be that it is also possible to have no respect for anyone, including ourselves. A person with this attitude does not put himself beneath others but fails to recognize that some behavior is disgraceful for any human being to perform. So he sees nothing wrong with bestiality, perhaps, or with addicting oneself to a powerful narcotic. In this way, he lacks respect both for himself and for other people, rather than simply failing to respect himself as fully as he does others.

This objection will be most appealing to those who believe we have souls or Purposes quite distinct from any personal purposes or some other light within us, which we abuse if we act in certain ways. Those who do not share such beliefs may consider the objection fundamentally misguided. Resolving that dispute is not important to us here, fortunately: our aim is to see whether humility amounts to a lack of self-respect. It is plain that humility does not amount to the view we have been describing. It does not amount to a depraved conception of humankind, that is. Indeed, since the humble understand themselves rightly, it follows that they would not take a view of themselves and their species that is defined as badly mistaken. In short, far from this being a way in which humility might amount to a lack of self-respect, it would be yet another unappealing view that a humble person would know too much to take.

2

Consider next a different way of making an exception of yourself: not morally but emotionally, so to speak. Here you do regard the behavior as mistreatment even when directed toward you, but you reserve your anger and indignation for occasions when someone else is the victim. Suppose your friend Charles is a terribly rude person, in a rather indiscriminate way. When he is churlish toward others, it annoys you and sometimes upsets you more deeply. When he acts this same way toward you, though, you have no emotional reaction at all.

You do acknowledge that it is wrong of him to treat you this way, and you would not necessarily tolerate such behavior from just anyone. So, this is not merely another case of thinking something is misbehavior when directed at others but a perfectly legitimate way to treat the likes of you. Still, it is only when someone else is Charles's victim that his rudeness gets to you, emotionally. So, it seems as if your moral disapproval were some pallid ghost of the real thing, as if you had come not to care about yourself as you should. If you are right to be upset on behalf of these others, should you not be upset on your own behalf as well? Is this yet another way to lack self-respect?

Let us consider the matter more closely. We are picturing you as someone whose reaction when mistreated is something like this: "Oh, that's just old *Charles*. He doesn't mean anything by it, and he'll probably be very sorry when he realizes what he has done. It's a real flaw in his makeup, and it used to make me mad, but now when he acts this way I hardly notice. I do get mad at him when he does these things to other people, though. They don't know him as I do, they don't know how to take it, and it is just as hurtful for them as it used to be for me."

My intuition is that this reaction can be self-respecting, but only for some kinds of mistreatment. It could excuse someone who has a temper, for example; or, someone who is a little awkward socially; or, someone whose mind wanders in what might be considered an insulting inattention to those around him. In those instances, the reaction amounts to a generous-minded tolerance of this person's foibles. That generosity may not be something anyone is obliged to extend to the Charleses of the world, perhaps, but doing so does not seem necessarily disrespectful of oneself, either.

Part of the reason tolerance can be self-respecting in these cases is that the behavior is not exactly the same when it is directed toward you as it is when directed toward others. It is the same in some ways—whether he is speaking to you or to others, Charles shouts and uses the same bad language, let us say. Still, when he treats you this way he knows he is doing it to someone who is not especially distressed by these outbursts. He has your history together as evidence of that. Whereas, when he acts this way toward new acquaintances, he does not know any such thing: they might very well be hurt by it, for all he knows. So his outbursts toward them are reckless in a way that his outbursts are not when directed toward you. That means your tolerance is not a way of taking exactly the same behavior lightly when it happens to you and seriously when it happens to others. This conclusion undercuts the claim that you must be failing to take yourself as seriously as you think others should be taken, showing thereby a lack of self-respect.

But tolerance also has moral limits, presumably. There are foibles you should not tolerate, that is, if you have any self-respect. If you do tolerate them in someone you are giving this person too much leeway: even if you do not give others the same liberty, there is a lack of self-respect in your letting this one person treat you this way. For example, suppose that what Charles does is to hit people, sometimes repeatedly. Or, less dramatically, suppose that what is "just Charlie's way" involves ridiculing you in public, making fun of your ideas, belittling your hopes and prospects, and so on. You say, quite honestly, "It doesn't bother me any more, because I know this is just the way he is. It only bothers me when he does it to people who don't know him, who don't have my perspective."

The trouble here is that "Charlie's way" is thoroughly disrespectful. It fails to take you seriously. So, to accept it as just his way is to accept that you are not to be taken seriously. As with the pattern of flagrant adultery, it is difficult to see his behavior as the aberration of someone who really does respect the person he treats this way. The aberrations, it seems, would be any moments in which he appeared to respect you.

The broader point is that we cannot defend every case in which a person accepts what he considers mistreatment as a case of self-respecting, generous-minded tolerance of another's foibles. Specifically, the tolerance defense fails when you have insufficient basis for believing the wrongdoer really does respect you, so that the (admitted) mistreatment would be an aberration. By contrast, what goes to make the defense succeed is your ability to point to a history containing plenty of evidence that you are respected, despite the current episode; your ability to explain the current deviation, by reference, for example, to some special, temporary pressure that seems likely to produce the uncharacteristic behavior; and genuine remorse in the wrongdoer after the fact.

Evidence of these kinds does not mean that you have not been treated disrespectfully. Instead such evidence makes it plausible for you to think you are respected despite these episodes. Thinking you are respected permits you to tolerate the episodes without lacking self-respect. It permits you to tolerate the treatment without demoting yourself from the class of people who are to be taken seriously. To put it differently: the insistence on being treated with respect need not come to insisting that every action toward you evince this respect. It need only amount to there being limits to your tolerance. You can allow others to slip, in other words, without having your tolerance of these slips amount to considering yourself a proper subject for such treatment or a lesser creature than anyone else. Your tolerance can be instead a way of being generous to the wrongdoer, in a manner you might not wish to be generous to him in his offenses against others.

It might be objected, however, that this misdescribes tolerance in an important way. The idea would be that tolerance does not consist in ceasing to be put off when someone, once again, exhibits his unfortunate ways, as I seem to have suggested, but in accepting him in spite of them. The tolerant person simply takes a larger view, draws on the good things to be said about the person now misbehaving, and shrugs it off. The tolerant person *does* take offense; it is just that she does not make an issue of the misbehavior, as she would be entitled to do.

Take, for example, Isabel Archer's reaction to Henrietta Stackpole in *The Portrait of a Lady*. When Henrietta goes too far in her efforts to ensure that Isabel marries Caspar Goodwood, Isabel certainly takes offense: "Isabel made no reply; the sense of Henrietta Stackpole's treachery, as she momentarily qualified it, was strong within her. 'Henrietta's certainly not a model of all the delicacies!' she exclaimed with bitterness. 'It was a great liberty to take.'"[11] Indeed, Henrietta's lack of delicacy is typical of her, displayed on other occasions in her unabashed willingness to ask highly personal questions. On one such occasion, "Isabel looked at her companion in much wonderment; it struck her as strange that a nature in which she found so much to esteem should break down so in spots. 'My poor Henrietta,' she said, 'You've no sense of privacy.'"[12] Isabel's tolerance consists in being aware that these are only spots on Henrietta's otherwise estimable nature. Henrietta has a very good heart; indeed, of the eight or so characters vigorously striving to direct Isabel's life, she is the only one without an ulterior motive of any kind. Isabel tolerates her faults in the light of that. She makes no large issue of the misbehavior, that is. She restricts herself to initial feelings and a few well-chosen words, even though she would be within her rights to do something more dramatic.

That is a different process than the one described earlier in connection with tolerating someone's bad temper or absent-mindedness: there, the victim had reached a stage of taking no offense at all. Now, suppose that Isabel's reaction were the accurate model of tolerance, with the earlier discussion merely depicting what it is to become inured to mistreatment. One might then try to revive Murphy's thesis that a self-respecting person always takes offense when mistreated, along the following lines: offense must always be taken initially, though it can be self-respecting to do little or nothing more than that (in the light of the offender's other virtues).

This is certainly a possible view to take of mistreatment, tolerance, and self-respect. And it does isolate one kind of tolerance: the kind in which we are distressed but, more or less, hold our peace. Moreover, it is plausible to say that when we are very badly mistreated, to react any *more* tolerantly than this would cast some doubt on our self-respect. We ought *at least* to take initial offense when we are seriously wronged, it seems. But there are also more minor forms of mistreatment, and to take even initial offense at them seems a bit stiff-necked: think of the person who cannot take a joke if it goes even a little too far. The boundaries between the acceptable and the unacceptable can be vague, and a little generosity when they are overstepped is not the same as meekly accepting a beating or a vicious slander as no worse than your due.

In addition, not all tolerance is like Isabel's, involving an initial flush of anger that one holds in check. Sometimes, it consists in merely registering that this other person's ways are not your own and finding the fact interesting, or even amusing. I do not mean to count this as tolerance when it is a person's response to something very damaging to him—then it would be a peculiar failure to take what happened as seriously as one should. But not every misdeed *is* damaging; as noted, some are more minor, and then the milder response can be tolerance. For example, suppose someone reacted in this way to one of Henrietta's overly personal questions, choosing not to take offense but only to find it amusing or fascinating that she should be so brash. Surely that would not betray a miserable conception of himself as a fit subject for mistreatment. She has only been rude, not horrendous; his reaction is not pitiful but only a way of exhibiting tolerance.

If so, we were not wrong, after all, to deny that self-respect always demands taking (at least initial) offense, regardless of how trivial the wrong or what the rest of one's relationship with the wrongdoer might be like. I have also suggested that self-respect does preclude making a negative exception of yourself in certain ways. For one thing, it precludes taking yourself not to be wronged by behavior you would take to wrong comparable others. For another, it precludes accepting without hard feelings what you recognize as misbehavior, when you have no adequate basis for believing that the wrong-doer really does respect you nevertheless. To do either of these is to demote yourself from a class in which you place others, without having an adequate basis for the distinction.

Humility could be charged with undermining self-respect if it inclined a person to do such things. But there is absolutely no basis for thinking it does, once we get past equating humility with low self-esteem and see it as a matter of having oneself in proper perspective. Hence there is no basis for thinking that humility (properly understood) involves a lack of self-respect.

3

Although humility does not involve taking yourself less seriously than you take comparable others, presumably it *does* involve not taking yourself *more* seriously than you take them. What would this come to, where reactions to mistreatment are concerned?

As a start, it is easy enough to imagine someone who is absolutely enraged when certain things are done to him, but does not even consider them wrong when they are done to others. That is a failure of humility, it seems plausible to say. Can we get further? From an objective point of view, a wrong of a particular kind is an equally bad thing to happen regardless who suffers it. Humility requires acting accordingly, not as if it were a worse thing when it happened to oneself. But what exactly does this require of a person?

A first answer is that it requires us to feel just as badly on behalf of others as we do on our own behalf. That is, if you were to learn that some stranger had been cheated or assaulted or whatever, you should be just as indignant on that person's behalf as you would be angered if these things had happened to you. Otherwise, the reasoning goes, you would be acting as if these events were more important when they happened to you, and thus as if you were more important.

This answer will not do. Taken one way, it is impossibly demanding. Your natural tendency is to be far more upset on your own behalf. Suppose you were to try to adjust by becoming more angry on behalf of strangers, so that you burned as brightly for them as you now do for yourself. A single perusal of the daily newspaper would leave you an emotional wreck. People are wronged all the time, sometimes monstrously. To feel as strongly about what happens to them as you now would if such things happened to you would mean that rage and sorrow would consume your life. The truth seems to be that reality is manageable only if we take a stranger's being mistreated *less* to heart than we would if we were the victim.

What about adjusting in the other direction? Instead of taking what happens to strangers more seriously, that is, what if you were to take what happened to you more lightly than people seem inclined to do and achieve consistency in that way? This might be more manageable, but its cost would be to weaken your reactions so greatly as to make them incongruous. Take, for example, rape and vicious assault, which are inflicted upon someone every few seconds. Given that you could not function if you were to feel anything like the rage and humiliation on their behalf that you would naturally feel if these things happened to you, how far would you have to tone down your reactions? How close to a shrug would you have to come, to achieve consistency? And then would you not have to laugh off entirely the lesser acts of dishonesty, cowardice, and unfairness in ordinary life, so as not to have your reactions to these out of balance to your new mildness toward dreadful misdeeds? Plainly, this route leads to the opposite of the attitude Jeffrie Murphy rightly recommends when he urges that "morality is not simply something to be believed in; it is something to be cared about."[13]

So much for the ways in which strangers might be as dear to you as you are to yourself, at least as far as wrongs befalling them are concerned. Neither is remotely plausible, it seems. If humility requires them, so much the worse for humility. But is it really a failure of humility, if you are more special to yourself than other human beings are to you? Perhaps it is not that what happens to you must be no more important *to you* than what happens to strangers but only that you must not take it to be more important *to the universe*, so to speak.

It would work this way: what is needed is that you take the victim of a particular wrong (whoever he or she is) to be entitled to a certain rough level of hard feeling. The stranger who was cheated is not entitled to as much outrage from you as you would feel if you were the victim, but he is entitled to be that outraged himself. This is as opposed to thinking that others make too much of what befalls them, even though you would wail every bit as loudly if you were the victim. Then you *would* be acting as if the wrongs were more important when they happened to you, it seems, and this would be a failure of humility.

There are further elements. A different part of taking something to be a wrong is to think that various other people should be distressed on behalf of the victim. How distressed they should be will depend in part on their relation to him. The properly humble attitude is not to expect people to be any more distressed at your misfortune than you would expect like people to be on behalf of someone else. This is as opposed to thinking utter strangers should be outraged when one of life's small indignities befalls you, for example. The presumption again is that you are no more significant intrinsically than anyone else.

If this is what humility requires, at least it begins to seem humanly possible to be humble. That distinguishes being humble from being as emotional about strangers as we normally are about ourselves. Nor would this humility require systematically numbing your feelings until they were ludicrously inappropriate to the wrongs that occasion them. You would be free to take what happens to you quite strongly. It is only that you would not expect that everyone else must give you the same place in their hearts that you hold in your own.

This approach permits the humble person to resent mistreatment, of course. It does not take humility to require that we never take offense, as does the view that we are all worthless. Nor does it join Murphy in thinking there is "almost necessarily" a lack of self-respect in anyone who takes no offense at an episode of mistreatment, or even a pattern of mistreatment. As noted, such equanimity might express anything from a false moral view to a reasonable tolerance of the wrongdoer's personal failings. There is nothing in humility that militates against these, any more than there is anything in humility that militates against self-respect.

4

I have argued that, to a certain extent, humility consists in taking what happens to you to be no more important intrinsically than it would be if it happened to someone else. If so, mistreatment calls for no stronger a reaction when you are its victim: not from the victim, not from the wrongdoer, not from the police, not from strangers, and so on. That is at least part of what it is for the event to be no more important.

I think this same point applies to the question of forgiving those who have done you wrong. If so, the trick would be not to take the wrong to call for any more hard feelings toward the wrongdoer, when it happens to you. Bishop Butler, in his sermon "Upon Forgiveness of Injuries," seems to offer similar advice: "In a word, all these cautions, concerning anger and self-love, are no more than desiring a man, who was looking through a glass, which either magnified or lessened, to take notice, that the objects are not in themselves what they appear through that medium."[14]

Specifically, Butler believed that almost all the harms we do to each other happen through ignorance, inadvertence, or self-absorption, rather than through malice. He may well have been right about this; he also thought that this fact ought to encourage us to forgive each other. Mistake, inadvertence, self-absorption, he said, "we ought all to be disposed to excuse in others *from experiencing so much of them in ourselves.*"[15]

Why would that follow? The odds are that we are not this hard on ourselves for our own such missteps. Probably we do not focus our attention on them to the same extent; probably we let up on ourselves more readily. Yet here, when someone has treated us in this way, we want to hold her feet to the fire. We do not want her to think this is something she can do and be forgiven for if only she is sorry and apologizes (though we do think of it this way when we have done it ourselves). Instead, we want her to understand and appreciate the enormity of what she has done. Similarly, since we are the victim, we think the victim is entitled to take what happened very seriously; if we were the wrongdoer, we would consider such carrying on excessive. This asymmetry does amount to a failure of humility, it seems.

But what if someone did not favor himself in these ways? What if he were every bit as hard on himself for slips and inadvertencies as he was in not forgiving others? He would be in for a very unhappy life, I should think. He might also lack humility in a different way. To expect something of someone is to assume that this person can do it—"ought" implies "can," as the saying goes. Hence, to expect a great deal of yourself is to assume that you have great ability. That assumption can exaggerate your potential so greatly as to constitute a failure of humility. For example, the man we have imagined might believe himself to be capable of virtual perfection, despite regularly failing to achieve it. He is simply not the person he takes himself to be, and it is unhumble of him to think otherwise.[16]

The idea is that there can be a certain lack of humility in having extremely high expectations of oneself, as, it seems, a person would if he expected himself never to err. If so, we should suspect a lack of humility in anyone who refuses to forgive others for the minor missteps he regularly commits himself. Perhaps he is easy on himself for that behavior, thereby considering it of greater cosmic significance when it happens to him. Alternatively, perhaps he believes himself to be a paragon who could fully avoid inattention and the like. Either would be a failure of humility.

Consider next a stranger whose car drenches you with mud because of her momentary inattention. She sees the mishap in her mirror and stops to apologize, insists on paying your cleaning bill, and so on. She begs you to forgive her for her moment's inattention, and it is clear that she is genuinely sorry.

You could forgive her, of course, but you are unmoved. In fact, you snarl, you bark, you make her very sorry she stopped. We have already noted a sense in which you may be exaggerating, either in pretending that this matters more when it happens to you, or in thinking of yourself as someone who avoids all such blunders. There is something else of interest here as well.

This woman did not have to stop, as we might say. Many of us would have driven on with at most a cringe and a wince, some with less than that, some even with a laugh. Very few would have been as solicitous as she. You could acknowledge that; you could shift your attention to her and see her as an unusually sensitive, gracious person whom you might quite like to know. Instead, you insist on retaining your focus on yourself as a victim.

There is something unhumble in that, I think, in the same way as paranoia is not humble. It is not that you exaggerate your virtues or accomplishments or worth. It is more a matter of exaggerating the extent to which life centers on you, and the extent to which you are unique. The early Woody Allen films exploit this point of view beautifully: the hero as victim, bemused at the way life singles him out for mistreatment. But really a great many of the sorts of things that happen to him happen to all of us, and when they happen they do not represent attention to the victim, their *point* is not to distress this person. Instead, they have no point at all, or they have some other point altogether. To think otherwise exaggerates one's cosmic position; that happens as well when one refuses to forgive people like the remorseful driver, it seems to me.

There are other contexts in which the refusal to forgive is like this. Suppose an intimate has wronged you but is now deeply repentant. In the classic description she is contrite, "bruised in the heart." Not to forgive her is to keep things focused on your being wronged, preventing the two of you from going beyond it. The relationship screeches to a halt; you freeze time at this one particular moment. It might be that the relationship should end, of course, or that what she did was so dreadful it should dominate your thinking about her. The point here is that this reaction can also exaggerate the importance of what she did.

The variables seem to be how bad a thing it was, how long ago it went on, and against what background of behavior toward you. To put it another way, it can be time for you to let up on her, because what she did was not so bad and because there is considerable other evidence of genuine respect for you. If so, to continue to dwell on her misdeed would make too much of it and of yourself, like someone's believing he should stay on stage when it is time for the show to continue.

There turn out to be several ways in which refusal or inability to forgive can be a failure of humility. One way involves taking wrongs to matter more when you suffer them than when they happen to others, or believing that you could avoid such missteps yourself. Other ways involve taking the world to be actively hostile toward you rather than largely indifferent, or insisting that what befell you must bring all else to a halt for far longer than it merits. All are ways of exaggerating your own importance. Humility does not demand that we always forgive, but it does demand that we forgive at times like these.

3

COMPASSION

The world is a place of utter misery for those who live in its more inhospitable parts. The leading such locale was Bangladesh, when Peter Singer wrote about "absolute poverty, with its hunger and malnutrition, lack of shelter, illiteracy, disease, high infant mortality and low life expectancy."[1] He rightly called this "life at the very margin of existence," and pointed out that it was all life had to offer, for "something like 800 million people—almost 40% of the people in developing countries."[2]

More recently, the continent of despair has been Africa rather than Asia, through a combination of drought, inadequate reserve and supply systems, civil war, and vicious politics. In Ethiopia, six million people face starvation.[3] One in every six Ethiopian babies dies in infancy: some as orphans, some in the arms of a helpless parent.[4] In sub-Saharan Africa more generally, parents lose ten times as many babies as North Americans or Europeans do.[5]

Television has given us images to attach to these numbers. We have seen the numberless multitude camped silent and helpless; the babies so motionless that their faces swarm with flies; the bloated, stick-legged children on the edge of

45

starvation. We have seen the suffering as clearly as one can see it, from our comfortable distance.

Against such misery, some Western lives seem shamefully profligate. For example, the *New Yorker* advertises custom-made suits "beginning at $1250," and gold wristwatches at $7500 for the lady's and $9500 for the gentleman's.[6] The suit is roughly twelve times the annual income of the average Ethiopian; the wristwatches are seventy and ninety times, respectively.[7]

Of course, suits and watches like these are not sold to the likes of you and me. Still, even you and I are incomparably better off than those in absolute poverty. We have closets full of clothing, refrigerators and cupboards stocked not with essentials but to our tastes, machines to lighten our work, and electronic devices to entertain us. We have, in short, incomparably more goods and wealth at our disposal, and a far wider choice of lives we might lead if we wished. We have and can do much; they have virtually nothing, and they can do little but suffer, endure for a time, and perish.

So what? Suppose I heard no call in all this. Suppose, in fact, I found it utterly boring; suppose it simply did not interest me, unlike the various plans, projects, and entertainments on which I spend my time and efforts. Would that be a lack of humility on my part? Would it exaggerate the relative importance of my being a professor, or my having a week at the beach; or my dressing to my taste, say; and, thus, would it exaggerate the relative importance of me?

At the other extreme, I could make it my life's work to ease the suffering in the lives of these distant strangers. I could give up my career and my ordinary life and direct my every effort toward helping them. If I followed this course, it seems likely that I would do considerably more good in the world than I do now. Is that the only way not to take myself more seriously than I should? Or would it be enough just to send a check somewhere, from time to time? Or perhaps not just to send the checks but also occasionally to do volunteer work for some worthy cause?

In short, what does humility require of you by way of compassion, if you are a fortunate person in a world so full of misery? Two things, I argue: a certain consistency between your compassion for others and the way you expect your own troubles to be treated; and freedom from self-absorption.

1

We can draw here on a point from the preceding chapter, where the question was how humility would incline a person to react when mistreated by someone. It emerged that humility does not preclude being more greatly distressed when we are mistreated ourselves than we would be if someone else were mistreated in that same way. For example, it is not a failure of humility for you to be more upset when your friend betrays you than you would be if my friend were to betray me, or to take news stories about assault or rape much more lightly than you would take being assaulted or raped yourself. In short, it is not unhumble to care more about yourself and what befalls you than you do about others.

What humility does preclude is (roughly) taking it that you (somehow) matter more intrinsically. It does not preclude your mattering more to yourself; it precludes your believing that you matter more, period. This latter, unhumble belief would be reflected in your acting as if a wrong should cost the villain more dearly when you are the victim or should be of greater concern to others or entitles you to react in a way you would consider excessive if the victim were someone else, and so on. Those are ways of taking the wrong to be a worse event, objectively speaking, *because it happened to you*. It is not, and so this elevation of oneself is a failure of humility.

A similar point applies to compassion, I want to suggest. The consistency that humility requires in our compassion, however, is somewhat harder to characterize than the consistency it requires in our response to mistreatment. The reason for this is that mistreatment is something we all experience: we are all on the receiving end of dishonesty, selfishness, unfairness, and so on, at one time or another. So it is easy to think how a person could exaggerate the importance of these when they happened to her. We need only recall our own lives, remember (sometimes with embarrassment) ways in which we have acted ourselves and ways we have seen others act, and examples will come to mind.

By contrast, none of us has experienced absolute poverty. So whereas we can reflect on times when we were cheated, we cannot also reflect on times when we were literally starving, when our babies were dying in our arms and no one who could save them would do so. We cannot consider whether our behavior at times like these is consistent with our behavior toward others in the same plight, because there have never been any such times in our lives. We cannot even think about how the starving people in our experience have acted, as we can think about how people we have known have reacted when they were cheated, for example. For, not only have we never been starving ourselves, we have never had any firsthand contact with those who are.

There is a way to construct the picture, however. Although we have been too fortunate to experience utter misery, or even to have it impinge on our lives to any considerable extent, we have all needed help from strangers on occasion. Think especially of help that it would have been easy for the strangers to provide, and that you clearly needed. Perhaps the regular travelers could have told you that the trains no longer left from the platform where you paced, and then you would not have missed your train. Perhaps someone in the lobby could have told you that your idea for a romantic moonlight saunter was likely to get you mugged, and so on.

Now, it could be that you have always been able to depend on the kindness of strangers in such situations. It could be that strangers have never failed to help you when you needed help, so that the memory of times when you have needed it fills you with good feelings toward humankind. More probably, though, there have been times when the strangers have acted as if you did not exist. There have been times when your predicaments have not interested them enough to divert them in the slightest. They have simply gone about their business, regardless of how obvious your trouble was, how serious, or how easy for them to relieve.

Such indifference can be taken with equanimity, but for many of us it adds to the misery. (How can they just ignore me? How could they just have passed me by?) As P. F. Strawson observes in a different context, it is important to us how others regard us.[8] Strawson has in mind our wanting not to be creatures people actively aim to injure. He would also have been receptive to the idea that we want to have our unhappiness matter to them—at least a little, not to be responded to as if we had no more feelings than a lamppost. To be roundly ignored when in obvious trouble is upsetting: it is as if we were invisible, or not sentient beings at all.

Not only is it upsetting: it may strike the person who is ignored as downright immoral, a failure of what W. D. Ross would have called a duty of beneficence. Or, if one admits that the strangers are "within their rights" to pass one by, their behavior might still be taken to show them to be pretty unappealing human beings: cold, self-centered, perhaps even a bit malicious. Not everyone will have had either of these reactions, I suppose, but they are common enough to be worth pursuing a bit further. What is interesting is that these feelings about strangers who ignore you in a time of trouble can coexist with complete indifference on your part toward those in similar predicaments. It is possible to be quite bitter about those who ignored you but still able to pass others by without a qualm, without a thought that you might not be acting as you should or that your own moral character might not be above reproach.

That combination of attitudes takes it that distress should be more compelling to strangers when it is one's own than when it befalls someone else. When I am the stranger and someone else is in trouble, it is all right for a stranger to be indifferent, on this view, but if our positions are reversed, this is an outrageous insensitivity to one's fellow human beings. Surely, that is the same failure of humility as taking it that a moral wrong should be more upsetting to strangers when it is done to me than when it is done to someone else. Each is a way of investing myself with an intrinsic importance that I do not have.

So far, though, this censures only inconsistency in one's attitude toward kinds of trouble in which one has sometimes been oneself. It means, for example, that it is unhumble to be inconsistent about people's need for directions, help with broken-down automobiles, and the like. The fact remains that few of us have ever been really badly off, like the people about whom Singer writes. How does the consistency requirement bear on that?

To see, let us suppose that when strangers leave you to miss your train or to wander into a dangerous neighborhood, you do think this shows serious flaws in their moral character. Surely you would be at least as upset with them if they could have saved you from much more *serious* trouble just as easily and were just as uninterested. If you are critical of indifference to your missing a train or risking a mugging, you would hardly be uncritical of indifference to your dying miserably of starvation. The fact that you have never been so imperiled is irrelevant; we can infer your attitude by considering what it is in these far lesser predicaments.

Once again, it is possible for there to be inconsistency between your expectations about how strangers should act if you were ever in desperate trouble, and your own conduct toward those who actually are in such trouble. In particular, it is possible to regard the actual sufferers as no business of yours, even though you are positively outraged by indifference toward you in your far lesser travails. Your outrage shows that you think strangers should take your being in desperate trouble very seriously indeed, if ever you were. Your indifference shows that you do not think another's desperate trouble matters very greatly, that is, you do not think it calls as importantly to strangers. This is the failure of humility we have been discussing.

The argument has been that indifference to strangers in terrible trouble betrays a lack of humility, if one also takes a dim view of strangers' indifference to one's own lesser predicaments. Most of us do take this dim view, I believe. Moreover, we think the view is perfectly justified. We expect our friends and acquaintances to commiserate with us, once we tell them how the strangers let us down. Accordingly, most of us would lack humility if we were indifferent to the serious suffering of strangers.

Indeed, most of us would be inconsistent (and thus unhumble) if we were not considerably moved by such people. For, most of us think that strangers should be considerably moved by us, even in our far lesser predicaments (and, hence, that they should be at least this concerned if we were ever in very serious trouble). The precise degree of compassion that humility requires of a particular person in this way will depend on how seriously he thinks his own troubles should move others. We differ in that. Thus, humility's demand that we be consistent will require more compassion of some than of others.

Imagine next someone who is perfectly consistent, but whose consistent view is that a stranger's troubles impose no moral claims on another stranger, regardless of whether it is she who suffers or someone else. Admittedly, she is a little annoyed when strangers refuse to help her. She regards this annoyance as without moral basis, however, like being angry at someone who has bested you in a fair competition. Again, she does want help when she is in trouble, and she would certainly want it if her trouble were very serious. But, again, she does not regard refusal to help her as morally wrong, or even as showing moral flaws in those who refuse to help. Thus, although she is herself indifferent to strangers in trouble, she does not inconsistently think that things matter more when they happen to her.

Therefore, she is not unhumble in the way just discussed. Is there a different way in which she lacks humility? There certainly is, if her view is part of a broader picture of herself as so capable that she will never need kindness, for that would surely exaggerate her powers. There is a deeper question, though, about whether the view that a stranger's troubles are of no moral interest to another stranger is itself unhumble. The question is whether others should matter to us in a way this view says they need not. The question is whether there is a lack of humility in being this self-centered.

To answer this we must understand compassion, since the hypothesis is that our woman is self-centered in lacking sufficient compassion for her fellow human beings. I focus first on what it is to have compassion for someone on a particular occasion, on what I call "occurrent" compassion. From there I describe what it is to be a more compassionate person or a less compassionate one, that is, more readily disposed to occurrent compassion or less so. That equips us to consider the effects of humility on this disposition and, finally, to consider whether the woman I have described is hardhearted in a way that betrays a lack of humility.

2

As Lawrence Blum has pointed out, to feel compassion for someone involves taking this person not just to be less well off than he might have been but to be in genuine distress: to be in a condition "relatively central to a person's life and well-being, describable as pain, misery, hardship, suffering, affliction, and the like."[9] Thus it is the homeless and the starving who arouse our compassion, not those, for example, who have merely run out of chewing gum or forgotten their homework. For them we might have sympathy, of course, but to say we felt *compassion* for them would be to speak ironically, as if their troubles were serious rather than petty.

Believing that someone is in serious trouble isn't all there is to feeling compassion for this person; that almost goes without saying. You must also be moved on his behalf, as opposed to being indifferent to him, or pleased that he has fallen upon such hard times or delighted that you are so much better off or simply fearful that it might happen to you at another time.[10] The usual effort to say what more there is to compassion emphasizes feelings: the feelings of the person who is in trouble and the feelings you have for him. Lawrence Blum puts it this way:

> As the etymology of the word suggests, compassion involves "feeling with" the other person, sharing his feelings. In one sense this means that the subject and the object have the same feeling-type: distress, sorrow, desire for relief. But in a more important sense the feelings are not the same; for the relation between their subjects and their objects are [sic] different. The focus of my neighbor's distress is *his own* homelessness; the focus of my distress in having compassion for him is *my neighbor's* homelessness (or his distress at his homelessness). This can partly be expressed as a matter of degree. My neighbor suffers; in "suffering with" him there is a sense in which I suffer too, but my suffering is much less than his.[11]

Here the feelings of the compassionate person are taken to be (roughly) "the same as he is having, only a smaller portion." I think this conception is mistaken in several ways.

Consider first the idea that those for whom we have compassion must themselves be suffering. Imagine that you have just heard some terrible news about an old friend: her youngest son has the worst form of leukemia. Medical treatments for it will be dreadfully painful for the child, incredibly expensive, and, worst of all, they will offer only a very slim chance of saving his life. You think of that poor little boy, and then of your friend, how she must be feeling and how her life will be shattered. The thoughts literally make you weep for them both, and you agonize over how you might be of any help.

In the midst of all this, the telephone rings again. This time, it is the best possible news: that story about your friend was entirely false. What a relief! You were so upset, so worried; how wonderful that the whole time they were living their normal, happy lives.

Now, does the happy ending to this story mean that you were not feeling compassion for your friend and her son during the hours when your heart ached for them? Surely not. At worst, it means your compassion was misplaced, that it was not called for, not that it was not compassion at all. Accordingly, compassion is not a matter of sharing the feelings of the person for whom one has compassion, since here there were no feelings to share.

At most, to have compassion is to feel for someone who would be suffering if her situation were as one envisions it. That alone is enough to dispel any picture of compassion as a spooky, direct contact with the emotions of others, a way of reading their minds—or, better, their hearts—and sharing what is there. This is not the right picture, since we can have compassion as long as we just believe that someone is in a very bad way.

What about the contention that at least the person who has compassion must have emotions herself, that she must feel for the poor soul she takes to be in distress? That certainly fits the standard case. Consider, though, the passerby who comes upon a terrible accident and immediately gets a grip on himself, as we say. He forces himself to stay calm, that is, because he believes an emotional reaction would render him useless to the people who need his help. Suppose he manages to carry this off, going immediately to the aid of the various people strewn about.

Our man is calm, albeit tense and grimly focused, and entirely free of the emotions that would wrack you or me on such an occasion. Accordingly, if by saying that compassion is an emotional reaction we mean that it involves occurrent feelings, on that analysis our man does not have compassion for the people he helps. But surely we do not want to say he lacks compassion for them, in the sense of being indifferent to their troubles. Nor is he the Kantian figure Blum disparages, who goes to their aid out of some abstract sense of duty.[12] His calm is self-imposed, and he imposes it for the sake of these individuals, the better to help them. He is calm because he cares about them, not because he does not care about them or because his eyes are fixed on the moral law.

If, as it seems, this is a second way of having compassion for someone, then although standardly the experience is rich in occurrent emotion, it can also be unemotional by force of will. That may be the attitude prized by some medical professionals, who want to avoid getting emotional about their patients without also ceasing to care about them as individuals, as the saying goes. In fact, adopting this attitude, as opposed to dealing with an isolated incident, may not be an especially healthy way to conduct an entire professional life. It may not even be in every patient's best interest: some patients would willingly trade a measure of professional efficiency for the realization that these people *felt* for them, that they had reached the physician or nurse emotionally. It makes one feel more of a human being and less of a technical problem. Those are other matters, however; here the suggestion is only that there might be unemotional compassion, as well as the kind that is definitely an emotional experience.

Be that as it may, suppose we return to the compassion that has an emotional tone: compassion in which one person is moved, emotionally, by the perception that someone is in a very bad way. Precisely which emotions the compassionate person will experience appears to depend on several variables, including what kind of trouble she takes the other person to be in, both in terms of how bad she thinks it is and how amenable to relief. Her own style in coping with difficulties might also have a bearing: for example, she might be inclined toward stoicism and therefore be less sympathetic. Her relationship with the sufferer, if any, might affect how badly she felt. For some, so would her views about whether the suffering was this person's own fault and whether its relief was her responsibility; others seem indifferent to such things, reacting only to the fact that this person is in trouble.

These factors would determine how sorry a person was (from mildly so to devastasted), how worried (from concerned through anxious to frantic), how frustrated over inability to help and angry at those responsible, and so on. Presumably, not everyone who feels compassion for a particular individual feels exactly the same thing. Nor does anyone feel the same way every time he or she has compassion for someone. Nor, finally, does it seem that the compassionate person is limited to feelings of the same type as the sufferer or that her feelings must be less intense than his, despite Blum's assertions to this effect.

Despite these variables, there is this much commonality to the emotions of the compassionate: none of these emotions is an enjoyable or even a restful feeling. To put it another way, people in such states want to get out of them. One strategy for doing so is to divert oneself from the source of the feelings; another is to try to *fix* things. Thus, a person who is unhappy about her work may avoid it as assiduously as possible; or, she may try to fix what is upsetting about it. In the same way, if she is upset by the perception that someone is in grave distress, she may deal with the matter either by putting it out of her mind—crossing the street, refusing to look, refusing to think about such things—or by going to the person's aid.

The emotions are genuine either way. But, of course, avoidance is not a compassionate reaction, in the cases described. The person who has compassion is the one who wants to help the poor devil, not the one whose whole motivation is to get away from something so nasty and upsetting. Moreover, to say that compassion involves an inclination to help the person taken to be in trouble does not mean that the compassionate person will always provide the help. The inclination to help will not be his only inclination, for one thing, and it will operate in the context of his beliefs about what is possible and appropriate. Moreover, it will itself be more or less strong, more or less easily overridden by these other considerations.

In summary: to feel compassion for someone is to believe this individual to be very badly off, and to be moved either to certain negative emotions of one's own and a disposition to help him, or to suppress those emotions the better to help him. The initial belief can be true or false, well founded or relatively unsupported. The particular emotions to which one is moved (or, moved to suppress) will depend on special features of the situation and on one's own personality, but they are some variety of sorrow, distress, anxiety, worry, frustration, anger, and so on. The disposition to help may be more or less strong and may or may not lead to action.

3

So much for what it is to have compassion for someone on a particular occasion. Now to consider compassion as a quality of character: what it is to be an especially compassionate person, or an especially hardhearted one. Presumably, such terms refer to how easily one is moved to have the feelings and dispositions we have been discussing, and how deeply one is moved when this does happen.

By how easily a person is moved I mean, in part, how serious the trouble must be. First, the more dire a sufferer's predicament must be before a person has any sympathy or wants to lend a hand, the less compassionate he is. Second, a person is less easily moved—and thus less compassionate— the more vivid and insistent a presentation of the suffering is needed in order to reach him. Some people are highly attuned, so that mere hints will get their attention, while others are relatively uninterested, so that the indications must be more insistent.

By analogy, a person would be more afraid of snakes if any mention of them were enough to make him uncomfortable, less afraid of snakes if the descriptions had to be especially vivid or accompanied by pictures, still less so if he were afraid only when there were snakes in his physical presence, still less so if he were all right until the snakes in the room were unconfined, and so on. Similarly, a person is more compassionate the more easily she is moved to unhappiness by the suffering of others, less compassionate the more obvious the suffering has to be.

The other measure is the depth of the compassion to which one is moved. Some people will go to much greater lengths than will others to help a person or an animal in trouble, sacrificing things of much greater value to them. Similarly, some people reach less readily than others the conclusion that there is nothing anyone can do, or that it would be inappropriate for them to help. Moreover, having reached this conclusion, some are more greatly frustrated than others, or more deeply saddened: here, too, we show how bad a thing it is for us that this other party is badly off. The more strongly a person is moved on a particular occasion, the more compassionate she is, other things being equal.

Let us combine these two variables and imagine two people who each read the following sentence: Three-quarters of the farmers in Poland do not own tractors. The first reader is terribly upset on behalf of the farmers of Poland, so much so that she is willing to sacrifice a great deal to make their lives less difficult. The second reader also believes that farming without a tractor is a hard life, but he can read the same sentence with virtual indifference. In fact, our second reader would be relatively unmoved if a starving child staggered up to him in the street and begged for help. "Someone should do something about this sort of thing," he would think, "but it certainly isn't any business of mine."

The idea is that the first reader is much more compassionate than the second. The difference between them is one of being easily moved to deep feelings, and being difficult if not impossible to move more than slightly. The first reader is greatly moved by rather undramatic indications of hardship that is considerable but by no means desperate; the second is only slightly moved by very vivid and insistent demonstrations of much grimmer misery.

In terms of this analysis, the question how compassionate a person should be is this: How easily should a person be moved by others in apparent distress, and how deeply? That is a prodigiously difficult question, in my opinion. Luckily, my own question is slightly different, and somewhat more manageable, roughly: How compassionate would a person be, if he were properly humble; that is, how readily and how greatly would a humble person be moved, given his disposition not to exaggerate his own importance? I argue against one answer to this, then offer another.

4

Consider the message in Peter Singer's work on famine and affluence. It is roughly this: those of us who have significantly more than we need to provide for our own basic human needs live immorally, if we spend that extra on ourselves rather than to rescue the desperate. Singer is not interested in humility, or in how much compassion we would have in our souls if we were humble.[13] His point of view can be recast easily enough, however, as a claim that we exaggerate our own importance when we act in this way. We act as if a trivial benefit to us were more important than an enormous benefit to someone else, the reasoning would go, and this is to act as if we were more important ourselves. Since we are not, that is a failure of humility on our part.

We ought instead to be moved much more strongly by the troubles of others. Specifically, we ought to be so alive to the needs of others that "it makes no . . . difference whether the person I can help is a neighbor's child ten yards from me or a Bengali whose name I shall never know, ten thousand miles away," and so deeply moved by each that I would make any sacrifice to help up to the point at which I do a comparable harm to myself (or to someone else.)[14]

Notice, first, how closely this view resembles one discarded earlier about the properly humble attitude toward the mistreatment that befalls others. Here, the central idea is that we should react, not to their being wronged, but to the distress of others as if it were our own. The distress should move us in the same way as if it were ours, namely, to do whatever is needed to relieve it so long as we do not do more harm than good in the process. To say humility requires that reaction to their misfortune is very like saying humility requires us to be as upset by someone's being mistreated as we would be if we were so mistreated ourselves.

The thesis about mistreatment was discarded, on the ground that it required something humanly impossible if achieved by taking others as seriously as we now take ourselves, or something incongruous if achieved by taking ourselves as lightly as we now take others. If those arguments were sound, we have good reason to reject the similar thesis about misfortune, as well. For, it would certainly be very strange if humility required us to find misfortune equally upsetting no matter whose misfortune it was, but permitted us to discriminate among victims of mistreatment.[15]

Moreover, just as it is impossible to be as upset over the wrongs done to others as you would be if you were the victim, it is equally impossible to be as vibrantly alive to the suffering our world contains as our version of the Singerian thesis says we should be. Think, for a moment, about how you would feel upon noticing your neighbor's child in terrifing peril for her very life, a scant ten yards away. Surely this is a very powerful experience, as powerful as any we are likely to have.

Now, first, imagine getting exactly this worked up about each of the children you know to be in similarly grievous conditions on the other side of the globe. Remember that there are literally millions of these children: according to Singer, every year there are five million children under five who die from the combined effects of malnutrition and infection.[16] Try to imagine being moved as powerfully by the misery of each of these as you would be by your neighbor's child's struggles for life in your very presence.

It is not just that you would be an emotional wreck if you were this tender, reduced to weeping bitterly over the hopelessness of it all. I do not believe you could be this tender at all, could feel this much. Human beings have emotional limits; there is nothing shameful or unhumble in anyone's not feeling in a way that exceeds those limits. And if, as I think, it is beyond our capacity to be this compassionate, there would not be much to be said for a thesis that we would be this compassionate if we were properly humble.

Second, remember Samuel Johnson's remark that the prospect of being hanged greatly concentrates a man's attention. Very intense feelings such as fear and concern are preoccupying, for as long as they last, diverting one entirely from other pursuits or, at least, severely reducing the attention one can devote to them. Moreover, intense feelings last for an appreciable length of time: imagine feeling *grief* for just an instant. It cannot be done: anything brief is not grief but something more shallow. (Nor, by the same token, is it *sorrow* or *distress*.)[17]

Accordingly, anyone who had the feelings involved in standard, deeply emotional compassion would be seriously distracted, for a considerable length of time. For that time, he would be unable to think about philosophy, for example, or to enjoy the tourist attractions or to concentrate on his novel. Small loss, no doubt, but he would also be distracted from silly games with his children and from the small doses of wholehearted doting on them that are so enjoyable to both sides. If his heart truly ached for the wretched of the earth, he just could not be this attentive parent.

Nor is our earlier dispassionate compassion more manageable. In dispassionate compassion someone puts powerful emotions temporarily on hold in order to concentrate his energies on helping those in need. Here the concentration would be permanent rather than temporary since, as Singer points out, the world continues to be full of people in desperate trouble. And, since the object is to focus as efficiently as possible on helping the needy, this too blocks attending wholeheartedly to lighter pursuits.

These arguments suggest that to be very compassionate is not an altogether good thing. It has its benefits, but it also has its costs. It might well be better to have less compassion in one's soul and more of some other things, such as responsiveness to those in one's daily life.[18]

We can further characterize the compassion that humility does require of us by noticing how very different the people are who do not live as Singer thinks we all should. Some are not much absorbed in anything. Others are thoroughly devoted to intellectual problems, for example, or to music or art, or to the fortunes of a few people about whom they care very deeply. It is conceivable that many of these people could do a great deal more good in the world if they abandoned these pursuits and devoted themselves to helping those who now perish in distant lands for want of what are literally the essentials of life. Their new careers would save lives, after all, and raise people from grinding misery to a bearable existence. No doubt there would be some cost to the history of mathematics or physics, to music or art, or to their loved ones. Would this not still be a bargain, though, from Singer's purely neutral point of view?

It seems so, and thus it seems that for Singer these people are not living as they should. Still, theirs are not selfish concerns, surely, not ways in which they take themselves too seriously—only, at worst, ways in which they take too seriously mathematics or physics, music or art, or certain loved ones. That matters: humility may require a proper perspective on oneself, but it does not require a proper perspective on everything, surely. We would overlook this, if we said that such people lacked humility *solely* because they did not spend their time as worthily as they possibly could.

To tell whether these other absorptions betray a lack of humility, we would need to know certain further facts. For example, someone who was greatly engrossed in physics or mathematics could harbor a belief that only she could solve the deep problems they pose; someone who toiled assiduously at the work at his office might believe that only he could do it properly. Clearly, such beliefs can be arrogant, but not every workaholic holds them: not everyone absorbed in his or her work is unhumble in this particular way.

Similarly, it is sometimes plain that a person places too much importance on the accomplishments toward which he is working, sacrificing all else to the work in question. His behavior is rather like taking excessive pride, in advance of having anything of which to be proud. There is the same conviction that very little compares in significance to his achieving the thing in question, the same assumption that he is justified in dwelling on it, the same assumption that others should set aside their (allegedly) lesser concerns. These convictions and assumptions can be just as foolish in someone working toward an achievement as they are in someone basking in one. Thus, absorptions are sometimes foolish in the same way as pride sometimes is. But, again, not every absorption in a project reaches this height of obsessiveness.

I have been suggesting that we can be absorbed in what we do without this betraying a lack of humility. Consider next someone who is rather uninterested in the suffering of strangers, not because he is absorbed in some project or in the fortunes of his loved ones, but because he is absorbed in himself. What fascinates him, the focus of his attention, are such matters as his appearance, his image in the eyes of others, how he is progressing up life's ladder, how he will entertain himself this evening, and so on. He is absorbed in these matters in the same way as a child might be absorbed in a game. He is difficult to distract from them, that is; he is virtually oblivious to calls to do something else, even though the calls are loud and clear.

I hasten to admit that there is nothing very crisp about the concept of being self-absorbed, or about the broader concept of being absorbed in something. Accordingly, there is no number of workouts a week or sum of money spent on makeup that sharply distinguishes narcissism from reasonable self-concern. Still, there is such a thing as self-absorption, and it does amount to taking oneself too seriously relative to other matters. To accuse someone of self-absorption is to say he should spend less of his time and energy attending to his hairline or his waistline or his wardrobe and more on something else: his children, perhaps, or his job or just something.

Alternatively, it may be that someone devotes too much attention not to his physical self and its comforts but to his personality or his moral character. What thoroughly engrosses him is what sort of person he is, whether he has this or that appealing trait: as the old joke has it, "But enough about me, let's talk about you: what do *you* think of me?"

In either variety, self-absorption differs from being absorbed in a profession or in the fortunes of loved ones, in that here it is oneself to which one gives too much importance. Thus, here there would be a kind of hardness of heart that would betray a lack of humility: namely, a kind that derives from taking oneself more seriously than one should. Again, to say this is not to accept the Singerian position, according to which we lack humility unless we devote ourselves to easing world poverty. For, devotion to that is not the only way to avoid self-absorption. Many who do not devote themselves to relieving poverty are absorbed in something other than themselves (and not unhumbly so), or in nothing whatever. Hence, when humility demands that we not be self-absorbed, it does not demand Singerian devotion to easing world poverty.[19] Exactly what it does demand is harder to say, but I make some points about it in the next section.

5

The discussion of Singer and of self-absorption was prompted by the statement of a particular moral view, according to which a stranger's troubles are of no moral interest to another stranger. That view offers the consistency humility requires: one who holds it appreciates that difficulties do not become more important intrinsically by virtue of their being one's own. Interestingly, it offers this consistency while permitting a person to be very hard of heart indeed. The question was whether this hardheartedness is unhumble in a different way, whether it amounts to what I have called self-absorption. We are now better able to see that it does not.

A small point first: certainly, the view that strangers are of no moral interest is one that a self-absorbed person would find congenial. For, this view would endorse the pursuit of self-interest, even in the presence of calls to compassion that are as loud and as clear as one cares to imagine. To hold the view is not the same thing as being self-absorbed, however. For, someone could hold it while really taking very little interest in herself, being instead thoroughly devoted to creating beautiful music, for example, or to the study of mathematics. So could someone who was fiercely devoted to her family, or someone who believed not only that strangers are of no moral interest but also that neither is oneself, the fortunes of a person's loved ones being the only proper subjects of interest. In short, to be indifferent to strangers and consider it perfectly appropriate for them to be indifferent to you is not the same thing as being self-absorbed, although it does permit you to be.

What sort of hardheartedness does humility absolutely preclude, when it precludes self-absorption? One element, already somewhat belabored above, is that what makes the person cool to the suffering of others must be some self-centered pursuit, else it is not *self*-absorption that she exemplifies. The other element is that the suffering she is ignoring must be presented loudly and clearly; otherwise, there is no self-*absorption* in her ignoring it. To be absorbed in something—including oneself—is to be difficult to distract from it, and that is shown only by the failure of serious efforts at distraction.

Essentially, a call to compassion qualifies as "loud and clear" insofar as the suffering it portrays is serious and vividly presented. Singer's example of the child drowning in one's very presence would certainly qualify: the trouble is about as bad as it can be, and the child's wild flailing and choked cries for help convey it vividly. The same holds for what James Rachels calls the "'Jack Palance' Argument," in which a child dying of starvation staggers into the lunchroom and collapses at our feet.[20] Anyone who took little notice on such occasions because she was attending to herself would qualify as self-absorbed, and therefore as lacking in humility.

What about someone whose daily path took her through streets full of people in great trouble, but whose interest remained focused on herself? If indifference to a single starving child in one's presence is self-absorption, would indifference to a great many of them be even greater self-absorption? I think not. A single sufferer stands out, in the same way as one sound stands out against silence, while many sounds of the same kind tend to blur into background noise. To get our attention something must differ from its surroundings; whatever is not different does not make a "loud and clear" call to us. That is as true of one more beggar as it would be of one more loud sound or one more patch of red against a red background. To be undistracted by such things does not signify absorption in what one is doing, unlike being impervious to the single shout, the one red light, the one person in trouble in one's presence. Accordingly, imperviousness to poverty that is all around one is not as significant as imperviousness to its sudden, stark intrusion into one's life.

What then of we who live in the prosperous West, and never actually encounter anyone in the sort of misery about which Singer writes? Can any call from a distance be sufficiently strong that failure to heed it could be evidence of self-absorption? I think so, but the specifics are debatable, in the same way as it is debatable whether we should consider a child absorbed in her game if she ignores a (clear) call from downstairs or only if she ignores one from her doorway or only if she ignores a shout from five feet away. No doubt, there are degrees of absorption, whether the absorption is in a game or in oneself, but we would be no better off if we focused on being greatly absorbed in something. These concepts are simply vague, and any attempt to make them precise will be arbitrary.

The vagueness does not render the concepts useless, however, but only restricts the uses to which we should try to put them. Although fine discriminations are arbitrary, we can still observe that it would be a mistake to count someone as absorbed only if she seemed not to hear very loud shouts from inches away. For the same reason, it would be a mistake to take a similar view about self-absorption. There are other calls that should penetrate, that should be clear enough, vivid enough, and desperate enough to distract a person from attending to himself. We can further characterize those calls by considering again the child who is playing a game.

Suppose we put various items in the child's field of vision, to see whether she will turn to them instead. If she is undistracted (or, only briefly diverted) by things we have reason to expect to interest her—a favorite teddy bear, a piece of candy—this will be more significant, surely, than if she plays on when tempted only by a blank piece of paper or a broken pencil. Playing on despite being offered what usually interests her is a sign of absorption in what she is doing.

Adults too have standing interests. For example, many adults pay great attention to show-business celebrities, and many pay considerable attention to most of the little children they encounter, even those who are total strangers. Imagine an adult who has both these characteristics, and who is engaged in some activity. Imagine that we try to distract her from this activity by pictures and prose about celebrities or about children. She is completely uninterested, however, or is diverted only briefly and then returns to her prior activity. As with the child at play, this would be a good reason for saying this person was *absorbed* in her activity.

Next, imagine that our woman is someone who lives a self-centered life, in a place where no one in very serious trouble ever actually crosses her path. She does, however, receive the kinds of charitable solicitations that have become fairly standard. I mean the kinds in which a celebrity appeals to us for funds, or a child who is very appealing but also very poor looks out at us imploringly, or a celebrity is holding a waif and both plead for our help. Our woman is impervious to these pleas, though; she takes scant notice of them before returning to her usual activities.

These episodes are good evidence that she is self-absorbed, it seems to me. For, what fails to distract her from attending to herself are matters that are usually of great interest to her. If so, since it is herself she finds absorbing instead, her imperviousness would be a failure of humility.

6

Because humility precludes being absorbed in oneself, I have argued, it excludes the grosser forms of heartlessness. It turns out to be unhumble for people like us to let someone drown in order to avoid getting muddy, as in Singer's example, or to go on with lunch when a starving child collapses at their feet, as in Rachels's example. It is difficult to say what further behavior is excluded, but there is good reason to believe that some representations of more distant suffering could not be ignored without self-absorption, assuming it was a self-interested pursuit that engrossed us instead. On the other hand, it would be wrong to think that we are self-absorbed (and thus lacking in humility) unless we spend ourselves doing the most good we can for people in great trouble.

Plainly, the stricture against self-absorption allows a great many different lives to be suitably humble. It requires some responsiveness to the troubles of others, but it does not say precisely for whose sake one must put oneself aside. Presumably, that will depend on which "loud and clear" calls are made upon one's compassion, and that will not be the same for every one of us. Certainly, there is nothing here that requires the objects of one's sacrifices to be the optimal beneficiaries of them, or that one must sacrifice to the point of doing oneself a comparable harm.

Humility's other requirement in this context is consistency between how seriously we take the misfortunes of others and how seriously we believe our own misfortunes should be taken. This too requires different things of different individuals. It obliges those who think others should take their being in trouble very seriously indeed to be more compassionate than those who think this is less momentous an event, in the history of the universe. Thus, the consistency requirement, like the requirement to avoid self-absorption, permits a variety of lives to be suitably humble in the compassion they contain.

4

ENVY
AND
JEALOUSY

How we should respond to those who are very badly off is clearly an important question. How we should respond to those for whom life is sweet is much less pressing, it would seem. After all, those badly off may very well remain so, unless someone offers them a helping hand; while those who are doing well do not seem to need any particular reaction from us, at the moment. They have fallen in love, or received a raise, or bought a new car, or whatever, and this is quite sufficient for their current happiness. Working out which way we ought to react to them is just not urgent, in the same way.

That is a point Bishop Butler makes, in discussing the following admonition from Romans, 12:15: "Rejoice with them that do rejoice, and weep with them that do weep."[1] As Butler notes, the admonition does not suggest that rejoicing with the fortunate is any less important than weeping with the unfortunate, even though that is how it might seem to us. He also observes that the admonition calls for considerably more by way of both weeping and rejoicing than is our usual practice. Ordinarily, we are not moved by everyone who is unhappy, or by everyone who is rejoicing, but only by some people; ordinarily, we do not find happiness of every kind infectious, or unhappiness of every kind moving.[2]

With those who are doing well, sometimes we are simply indifferent to their flourishing, especially when they are strangers and we see no connection between them and us. Other times, we have a darker reaction. We hear of someone's good fortune, and not only do our hearts not leap, they positively sink. We wish our colleague had not had that article accepted or had not received that handsome raise or, anyway, that not everything would go quite so well for him.

There is more than one basis for reacting in this way. It may be that the person who is flourishing is someone you intensely dislike. Then the news that he is doing well, the swine, hardly fills you with joy; in fact, it can ruin your whole morning. Or, after a tennis match, it may be that what makes this other party rejoice is her resounding victory over you. To join in her celebration would be unusually sporting, a sign of a generous heart. You might manage instead to regard the celebration as something to which she is entitled, at least—after all, she did win—but you might also be not even this good a sport. Finally, it is possible to react to another's doing well by becoming envious, or jealous: the two reactions on which this chapter focuses.

The ultimate question for us is what humility has to do with envy and jealousy. For example, is humility somehow proof against these, so that someone who was properly humble would never be envious or jealous of someone who was doing well? Alternatively, does humility incline one against some forms of jealousy and envy, although not against others? Or (as Friedrich Nietzsche might have said) is the relationship just the reverse, so that the humble are actually more inclined toward envy and jealousy, their very humility a sort of sublimated resentment of their betters? The first step toward answering this is to work out what envy and jealousy are, exactly.

1

Everything has fallen into place for your colleague. The college has granted his request for a sabbatical leave, and a supporting fellowship has come through. The scholars at his destination have extended a most cordial welcome. He is to have a year in a delightful, stimulating setting, with plenty of time in which to do his work. You would like to be happy for him. However, you cannot stop comparing his situation to your own, and a certain sourness afflicts you. The truth is that you are not happy for him, no matter what you might manage to say. The truth is that you are unhappy for yourself—sorry for yourself, as we sometimes say—and more than a little resentful toward him.

Does this amount to being envious of your colleague, or to being jealous of him? Offhand, it seems that either expression would serve equally well. And that raises a general question: if there is a difference between being envious and being jealous, what is it? Perhaps a different example will help: suppose you have a rival who is becoming the chairman's favorite. She is the one who gets the choice teaching schedule, the one whose advice the chair seeks and thoughtfully quotes to the rest of the department as if it were profound, and so on. This is all becoming a bit too much for you to bear. Over lunch, you entertain us with scurrilous, spiteful "explanations" of this new special relationship, and witty denigrations of your rival's merits. Shall we think of you as jealous? Or, as envious?

Again, either term might seem acceptable. Daniel Farrell offers an appealing way to make the distinction, however, in his excellent articles on jealousy and envy. Essentially, he suggests taking envy to be a two-place relation and jealousy to be a three-place one. "In cases of envy, there are just you and I, so to speak, and what you have and I don't. In genuine cases of jealousy, on the other hand, there are you and I and the person who is giving *you* what I want *that* person to give me."[3]

On this way of speaking you are *jealous* of your rival for the chairman's favor, not envious. For, what upsets you is the chairman's giving her the attention, esteem, and perquisites that you want the chairman to give you. By contrast, you are *envious* of your colleague with the wonderful sabbatical, not jealous, because what bothers you is just the difference between his lot and yours. You are not bothered by a third party favoring him over you, but just by how much better off he is about to be. We could change the example so that you were jealous, instead, by supposing that the college had granted him a sabbatical instead of you, and that this was what bothered you. Or, we could picture you as partly envious and partly jealous, by making you upset partly by his doing better and partly by his being favored.

As Farrell acknowledges, this way of distinguishing jealousy from envy is somewhat artificial. Often, we use the terms interchangeably. In particular, we often call jealousy what Farrell would have us call envy, as when we say someone is jealous of your new car or jealous of your good looks. For, when we say such things we do not mean that this person feels displaced from some third party's favor: there are just you and she, in Farrell's terms. His distinction covers a great many cases, though, and I use it in what follows.

Since in envy there are only two principal parties, the envious person's feelings have only two principal targets. One is the person envied, who often is resented or hated or feared or regarded with a certain hopelessness. The other is oneself; often the envious are also dismayed with themselves for their inferiority or impatient with themselves or angry with themselves, as well as envious of the rival.

Since in jealousy there is a third principal party, there is someone else about whom to feel strongly, and the emotional brew is somewhat enriched. Thus, disgruntled employees are sometimes upset not only with their rivals but also with the boss, and jealous husbands sometimes shoot not only their wives' lovers but also their wives. Whether a husband is more upset with his wife or with the other man may depend on whether he thinks of her as someone who freely chose to betray him or as a weak creature who was seduced by a cad. Which of those pictures he adopts might have more to do with his own psychology than with the facts of the matter, but that is another concern. The idea here is only to hint at how rich the emotions can be when the game has three main players rather than two.

Further analysis is complicated by another looseness in our usage. We sometimes make the following sort of remark: "You have such a lovely house—I'm truly envious!" In saying such things we aim only to pay a compliment. A different speaker might have said, "I really love your house!" or "Gosh—what a neat house!" if that were his conversational style.

Since these declarations of "envy" are compliments, we offer them perfectly cheerfully—or, at most, with a wry indication that our own dwelling is far more humble. There is no air of confession to the remark, no indication that the envy is something of which we are at all ashamed. Nor is our declaration of envy received as if something shameful had been admitted. Instead, the exchange is all bonhomie and good cheer.

That alone should make us suspect that these declarations of envy are not to be taken literally. Genuine envy, if Thomas Aquinas is right, is both a capital and a mortal sin. By calling envy a capital sin he meant that it gives rise to other sins; in the case of envy, to "hatred, tale-bearing, detraction, joy at our neighbor's misfortune, and grief for his prosperity."[4] Aquinas considered envy to be antithetical to the spirit of charity we should have toward our fellow human being.[5] But think of the example of being so struck by someone's house that you wished yours were as fine and wanted to tell this person so. That is simple admiration, it seems, and perfectly consistent with having all the good will in the world toward the person you "envy." So, it does not appear to be what Aquinas had in mind.

This suspicion is strengthened when we note that he counted envy as also a mortal sin: something so wicked that to die without having confessed it means eternal damnation. Dante was not much more tolerant: on his account, the envious are condemned to stay in purgatory with their eyelids sewn shut, while angelic types flutter overhead incessantly murmuring homilies about charity.[6] By contrast, again, we are not in the least ashamed of "friendly" envy, but express it quite cheerfully—and it is hard to see why we should be ashamed of it, since it amounts only to admiration and the willingness to pay a compliment. What a stunning reversal of attitudes this would be, if what we were so cheerful about were the same thing that Aquinas and Dante thought so dreadful. Better, again, to take it that they had something different in mind. Better to assume that genuine envy differs from simple admiration and is more than the wish that one were as well off as another, in some regard.[7]

To see what more it involves, notice first that to want something, even something you know you are not very likely to obtain, is not the same as being upset about your situation. For example, most of us would like to have a million dollars, and most of us know that we are virtually certain never to have this desire satisfied, but very few of us are upset about this state of affairs. By contrast, an envious person *is* upset. His situation bothers him.

As the envious person pictures things, some other party is quite definitely better off than he, and this is a bad thing. He thinks this other person has had an accomplishment or a piece of good luck that he himself has not had, or that she has some sterling characteristic that he lacks. This (believed) compound state of affairs is what occasions his distress: not the fact that she has X, or the fact that he does not have it, but the fact that she has it and he does not.[8] Finally, at least some of the bad feelings this generates in him are directed toward her; these feelings are the envy he feels for her.[9]

The feelings are not always the same. Sometimes we hate the people we envy; sometimes we are angry at them; sometimes we fear them a bit—all feelings occasioned by the perception of this disparity between them and us, I am suggesting. When it is a friend we envy, the hard feelings may be less dramatic: there may be only a momentary stiffening, a discomfort that was not there before, a subject that now makes us a little tense in connection with her. The general idea is that to envy someone is to have our feelings about this person affected negatively, because we believe he or she has some good thing we do not have ourselves.

That attitude, unlike "friendly" envy, is clearly very different from admiration. It is also very far from feeling charitable toward this person: from hoping good things come her way and being willing to sacrifice for her sake and giving her the benefit of the doubt and so on. So we can make good sense of Aquinas's condemning envy as antithetical to the spirit of charity, if we understand envy as suggested.

Since what occasions the envious person's distress is the perceived disparity between herself and the person she envies, in theory there are two ways for her distress to be relieved. She might acquire the desideratum herself (or, prove to have had it all along); or, the individual she envies might lose it (or, prove never to have had it after all). Envy thus can be a spur to very different attempts to eliminate the disparity: either by getting the thing for oneself, or by seeing to it that the other person loses it.

There are several less active strategies popular with the envious as well, designed chiefly to picture the apparent gap as less distressing than it seemed at first. Simple sour grapes is one variation: if it was not much of an accomplishment after all, perhaps the gap between us is not so great that I should trouble myself over it. When the other person's achievement is too substantial to be undermined in this way, the envious party might disparage the rival more broadly: "All right, granted he is brilliant, much more so than I, but he is so *odd*, how can anyone take him seriously?" Here the idea seems to be that I have compensating advantages that outweigh the respect in which the rival does, admittedly, have an edge: so that, again, it is not an edge that should upset me, given the larger picture. If I can convince myself of that, I can stop being envious.[10]

One further strategy is to convince yourself that the person you envy came by her advantage unfairly. She cheated; they gave it to her because she is a woman; she has friends in positions of power; and so on. If so, again it is not so much of an accomplishment with which to have to cope. When such complaints are perfectly outlandish, we are likely to tell the person he is "just envious" (or, to say this to each other after he has left our company). Sometimes, our analysis is right on the mark.

But there is also such a thing as genuine indignation. Here what upsets you really is what you see as the unfairness of it all, not the simple fact that she has surpassed you. Then to say you were "just envious" would be to pour salt in your wound. You are not envious; you are upset over a perceived injustice.

As we know, it is not always easy to tell whether someone is genuinely indignant or only envious. On the account being given here, that is because it is not always easy to tell exactly what is upsetting someone, or whether more than one thing is doing so. The person may even deceive himself about it to maintain a more attractive image in his own eyes. Or he may begin with envy, upset just by the disparity he perceives, and (the more he thinks about it) pass on to indignation over the unfairness of it all, as he convinces himself that an injustice has been done. Here, again, he is not just envious, but neither is he quite like someone whose sense of justice was the only thing offended from the start.

Such complications aside, the general argument I have been making is that envy consists in negative feelings toward someone that are occasioned by the perception that this individual has some good thing that we do not have. That analysis makes it plausible that envious people should behave in the ways we commonly do find them to behave: proclaiming that the grapes are sour or disparaging the person who has them or complaining that the grapes were obtained unfairly. The analysis also distinguishes envy from other negative reactions to someone's flourishing, such as righteous indignation.

It also distinguishes being envious from being upset because someone you intensely dislike is flourishing. Perhaps, for example, you have just heard that your worst enemy has been given an enormous raise. Although he still makes much less than you do, you hate to see it happen. It galls you to see him flourish—but that is not the same as being envious of him.

Nor is it the same, on the suggested account of envy. For, what makes you unhappy here is the (believed) fact that your enemy is doing well, not that he is doing well in a way in which you are not. You are not bothered by the compound state of affairs that would bother an envious person, that is, but by a simpler one.[11]

Finally, the account captures as well a subtler difference between being envious of someone who surpasses you, and being upset only with yourself. Suppose that when you learn that some acquaintance has done superbly well, you immediately think about your own shabby performance, and then about how basically inept you are and have been your entire life. The perceived disparity has occasioned some hard feelings, all right, but all of them are directed at yourself. This is not envy. It is depression and self-reproach.

So much for what envy is. Following Daniel Farrell, I take jealousy to differ in that it is occasioned not by the perception of a disparity but by the belief that someone is giving to another something you want that person to give to you. To be jealous is to have this affect negatively your feelings toward the (alleged) lucky recepient. Your feelings can include anger toward him or hatred or a hopelessness verging on dread or just a little discomfort about him. Now to consider what humility has to do with these reactions.

2

Let us begin with jealousy, the partial rehabilitation of which is a major project of Farrell's. As he notes, there may be nothing intrinsically objectionable about the desires at the heart of a person's jealousy. For example, to want your wife to be more fond of you than she is of anyone else or to want her to share her sexual favors only with you is hardly in a league with wanting to break someone's bones for the sheer pleasure of it. Moreover, being special to someone is deeply satisfying, quite apart from whatever ancillary benefits it might bring. There seems to be nothing necessarily improper about wanting either the satisfaction or the benefits.

Just as the desire for favored status can be unobjectionable, so can the reaction to the prospect of losing that status. If something you badly want is given to someone else instead, this seems quite likely to be upsetting. And, for you to be upset with the parties who are doing this seems perfectly appropriate. Taken altogether, this suggests that jealousy itself can be perfectly appropriate, a reasonable reaction to the frustration of an equally reasonable desire.[12]

So far, there is also no basis for expecting that humility would preclude our feeling jealous. To be humble, I have argued, is to understand yourself and your accomplishments sufficiently clearly that you are disinclined to exaggerate who you are or what you have done. Praise does not go to your head, that is; nor are you disposed to insist on more attention to your achievements or misfortunes than you would consider these to deserve if someone else were involved. Moreover, you are disinclined to mistake indifference to you for part of a subtle plot against you, you are not greatly self-absorbed, and so on. There is nothing in that makeup that would rule out wanting to be dearer to someone than anyone else is, it seems, or being upset with the lucky party if you proved not to be.

There is also unreasonable jealousy, however—several varieties, in fact. It will be interesting to characterize them, and then to see whether humility disposes us not to be unreasonably jealous, even if it does leave us vulnerable to reasonable jealousy. I will argue that this is indeed the case.

Think first of the classic jealous husband, who is troubled by his wife's even conversing with any "eligible" male, and whose definition of "eligible" is generous indeed. Her mentioning another man with approval arouses his darkest suspicions; heaven forefend that he should ever see a man make her laugh or touch her arm. In sum, he takes perfectly innocent encounters to be genuine threats to his relationship with his wife.

We can see the workings of baseless jealousy in Shakespeare's *Othello*, if we think of Iago, not as a villainous separate person who deceives Othello for reasons of his own, but as the Moor's own inner voice.[13] That voice doubts almost from the start that Desdemona's fascination with him will continue for long.

> Her eye must be fed; and what delight shall she have to look on the devil? When the blood is made dull with the act of sport, there should be, again to inflame it, and to give satiety a fresh appetite, loveliness in favour, sympathy in years, manners, and beauties; all which the Moor is defective in: now, for want of these required conveniences, her delicate tenderness will find itself abused, begin to heave the gorge, disrelish and abhor the Moor; very nature will instruct her in it, and compel her to some second choice.
>
> (act 2, sc. 1, lines 225–35)

That choice will be Cassio, the voice instructs him, for Cassio has exactly what he lacks himself.

> Now, sir, this granted—as it is a most pregnant and unforced position—who stands so eminently in the degree of this fortune as Cassio does? a knave very voluble. . . . Besides, the knave is handsome, young, and hath all those requisites in him that folly and green minds look after; a pestilent complete knave; and the woman hath found him already.
>
> (act 2, sc. 1, lines 235–48)

Once the seed is planted, its nurture is an easy matter.

> *Iago:* Ha! I like not that.
> *Othello:* What dost thou say?
> *Iago:* Nothing, my lord: or if—I know not what.
> *Othello:* Was not that Cassio parted from my wife?
> *Iago:* Cassio, my lord! No, sure, I cannot think it,
>   That he would steal away so guilty-like,
>   Seeing you coming.
>
> (act 3, sc. 3, lines 35–41)

As his inner voice reminds him, Desdemona has already shown herself to be a skillful and willing deceiver when she wants a forbidden lover.

> *Iago:* She did deceive her father, marrying you;
>   And when she seem'd to shake and fear
>   your looks,
>   She lov'd them most.
> *Othello:*   And so she did.
> *Iago:*   Why, go to, then;
>   She that so young could give out such a seem-
>   ing,

To seel her father's eyes up close as oak—
He thought 'twas witchcraft . . .

> (act 3, sc. 3, lines 209–16)

Once these doubts are in place, how are they to be resolved? Not by talking things over with Desdemona, since he has come to doubt her: how could he trust what she would say? But then what other evidence would he seek?

Iago: . . . how satisfied, my lord?
          Would you, the supervisor, grossly gape
              on,—
          Behold her topp'd?
Othello: Death   and   damnation!   O!

> (act 3, sc. 3, lines 401–3)

The idea of catching them in the act is nearly unthinkable. He does not want to see that; and anyway, they are hardly likely to be so careless. But if he is not going to see with his own eyes that she is faithless, and he cannot trust Desdemona's own testimony, he will have to judge by circumstantial evidence. He will have to attend to various signs and draw the logical conclusions. He is convinced he can do this fairly and that only the most compelling evidence will convince him of her guilt.

> . . . But yet, I say
> If imputation and strong circumstances,
> Which lead directly to the door of truth,
> Will give you satisfaction, you may have't.

> (act 3, sc. 3, lines 412–15)

He is deceiving himself, in a way captured neatly in a later exchange between Desdemona and Emilia, as they ponder Othello's ominous shift of mood.

> *Emilia:* Pray heaven it be state-matters, as you
> think,
> And no conception nor no jealous toy Con-
> cerning you.
> *Desdemona:* Alas the day, I never gave him cause.
> *Emilia:* But jealous souls will not be answer'd so;
> They are not ever jealous for the cause,
> But jealous for they are jealous: 'tis a
> monster
> Begot upon itself, born of itself.
>
> (act 3, sc. 4, lines 158–64)

A jealous person brings his suspicions with him and judges by those—the very opposite of the impartial judge he takes himself to be. The prejudicial effect is more powerful the more thoroughly he convinces himself that his judgment is fair, that he has put his suspicions aside and is being perfectly objective. In fact, jealous suspicions are rarely *tested* by such a process, so much as they are simply confirmed.

So it is with Othello. The handkerchief he gave Desdemona turns up in Cassio's possession, and though Othello never made its importance clear to her and there is an innocent explanation, he knows it means the worst. Cassio is overheard speaking derisively of a woman who loves him, and Othello knows this must be Desdemona—though he has no reason to think so. Counterevidence from Emilia is swept aside, though he has no reason to doubt it except for its not fitting the picture he has constructed. Desdemona herself is consulted only after the verdict has been reached, when her protestations can only be taken to add perjury to her sins.

Othello's jealousy destroys everything most spectacularly. While baseless jealousy is not, as a rule, literally fatal to both the jealous person and the object of his affections, typically it is powerfully destructive. Why, then, do people indulge in it? Since the roots of baseless jealousy are so thoroughly within the jealous person, and confirmation to this person's jealous eye is so inevitable, actually it is they who wreak their own destruction. Those who are prone to feel baseless jealousy are prone to spoil their own lives. Why someone should be that way is truly difficult to comprehend; certainly, the explanation is not accessible to the person himself through an easy introspection, as we may take this last exchange between Othello and his inner voice to observe.

> *Othello:* Will you, I pray, demand that demi-devil
> Why he hath thus ensnared my soul and
>   body?
> *Iago:* Demand me nothing; what you know, you
>   know:
> From this time forth I never will speak
>   word.
>
>   (act 5, sc. 2, lines 305–8)

In Othello's case, it seems plausible to take his problems to begin with his sense of himself as inescapably different from the others and therefore unreachably apart and separate from them. The differences are not imaginary: he is a Moor in a Venetian state, and he has heroic qualities that distinguish him still further from the others. The trouble is that even the woman he loves is not like him—no *one* is like him—she is, instead, one of *them*. He takes this to mean that she cannot truly and faithfully love him: he is not her kind, not the kind who could be the object of her true and faithful love, but someone irretrievably apart. She may seem to cherish him, but this can only be a brief fascination and must eventually be false, as she turns to some more suitable object of her feelings. With those thoughts, the destruction begins.

Perhaps there is often an inescapable loneliness at the heart of groundless jealousy. Perhaps, that is, it is often because the jealous person takes himself to be too alien for intimacy that he behaves in ways that destroy the intimacy or prevent it from the outset. If so, he arranges thereby to sustain his unhappy hypothesis, since it is through intimacy that we learn we are not so different in those deep and secret ways we think we are.

On other occasions it may not be a sense of being different that fuels baseless jealousy so much as a fear and half-belief that we are worthless and undesirable, and a constant expectation that those we care about will find others more appealing. After all, virtually everyone *is* more appealing, on this view. So, the inevitable is long overdue, and any allegedly normal interchange is probably either the beginning of the end or a part of something well under way already.

Whatever its ultimate sources, jealousy based in a sense of worthlessness might seem to have little to do with humility. After all, this kind of jealousy involves underestimating oneself, taking oneself to have much less to offer than one actually has. Clearly, then, a disinclination to underestimate oneself would protect against it. But I have argued that humility is (roughly) a disinclination to *over*estimate oneself; why that would protect one from this kind of jealousy is much less clear.

Recall, though, that humility is not simply the disinclination to overestimate oneself but a disinclination with a particular basis. Humility differs in that way from broad cynicism about all human beings—an attitude that also includes a disinclination to overestimate oneself. Similarly, it differs from simple ignorance of one's merits and from self-deception about them, even though, again, these too can include a disinclination to overestimate oneself. Humility consists instead in *understanding oneself so well* that one is disinclined to overestimation.

I am not speaking of *perfect* self-knowledge, I hasten to add. For one thing, humility comes in degrees, unlike perfect self-knowledge. For another, humility is attainable. The idea is that humility consists in having oneself *more* or *less* in perspective, and being disinclined for that reason to overestimate one's virtues or what one might have done or one's significance in the lives of others. That is why humility is a virtue, unlike ignorance, self-deception, or cynicism, and a virtue that can be present in the highly accomplished.

Since on this view humility involves having some reasonable grasp of what one is like, a humble man would not be so terribly wrong about himself as we were imagining the jealous husband to be. Put it this way: he could hardly understand his merits sufficiently to resist exaggeration without also understanding them sufficiently to realize he was not utterly worthless, or to realize he was not so crucially different from others. The jealous husband's causeless jealousy arises from the false belief (or, fearful half-belief) that he is utterly worthless. Othello's arises from an inability to see that he has features that can attract and sustain love. These are mistakes a humble person would know too much to make. So, humility is a barrier against jealousy of this unfortunate kind.

There is also a way in which baseless jealousy can become self-fulfilling. That is, the husband's unfounded suspicions and jealous rages can make him so repellent that his wife does indeed find someone else. Then at some point his jealousy is not without cause but perfectly appropriate: she really is giving to someone else what he wants her to give to him. Humility would prevent one's reaching this stage, however, since one would not be so wrong about oneself as to become prey to the baseless jealousy that starts the process.

Consider, finally, this slightly different variation of the jealous husband. Here it is not that he wants (perfectly reasonably) to be his wife's only lover and (unreasonably) takes innocent interchanges to show that he is not. Instead, what he wants is to be virtually the only person in her life, the only one who provides her with any pleasure or stimulation of any kind, the only one with whom she has a relationship of any depth. So he is jealous, not only of those he thinks might be her lovers, but of her mother, their children, her women friends, and so on. He is quite right to see certain interchanges as showing that he does not have the place in her life to which he aspires. It is the aspiration itself that is unreasonable and that makes his jealousy unreasonable.

Here again the standard explanation would be that the man is desperately insecure. If so, no humble person would have this affliction, for the reasons mentioned. Alternatively, it is (barely) conceivable that someone would really think himself so fascinating that his wife should have no interest in anyone else and could only be wasting her time. Such a person might find her interchanges with others upsetting, perhaps out of a bizarre paternalism. If he were capable of jealousy on such occasions, it would certainly be a kind to which no humble person would be prey.

3

This leads naturally to the concern that all jealousy is childish, that there is something inherently immature about jealousy as a reaction to losing out. The wish to be all things to someone does seem reminiscent of how some of us felt about our "best friend" when we were very small: we did not want this person to have other friends.[14] I suppose that severe self-doubt can also be childish in a way, in that it is part of normal maturation to learn that one has merits and that one's place in the affections of others is not constantly under threat.

However, I take Farrell to have shown that not all jealousy is like this. Instead, some jealousy is a perfectly sensible reaction to a genuine threat to a favored position that it is not unreasonable to desire. So described, there seems to be nothing immature about jealousy. The matter is worth a closer look, though: perhaps jealousy can be childish in a different way.

Consider again the desire to have a favored position. As Farrell points out, some such desires are unobjectionable, morally. Some of those unobjectionable desires are also perfectly hopeless, however. For example, imagine wanting to be first in the affections of some absolutely stunning movie actress. There is nothing morally objectionable about that, presumably, and conceivably it could grow to be quite an avid desire. Given the avidity of this desire, reports that this woman was sleeping with her costar might be very upsetting. Since the desire and the reaction are reasonable, the jealousy would not be childish, on Farrell's account.

But it *would* be childish, surely. It is exactly the kind of thing we would expect in an adolescent. If we found it in a grown man we would consider it pathetic, if not downright alarming (think here of John Hinckley's adoration of Jodie Foster). In what does its childishness consist, though? If the desire at its heart were itself childish, like a desire to put gum in someone's hair, we could say that whatever flowed from it was also childish, including the jealousy in question. But the desire to be the man in some actress's life is not childish in this same way. So, we shall have to seek a different account.

Let us begin with a point made earlier: there is a difference between merely having a desire and placing some importance upon satisfying it. If it is important to you to satisfy a certain desire, you will be willing to go to some lengths to do so, you will be especially pleased when you succeed—and, you will be especially disappointed when you do not. In contrast are your various mere preferences and more or less idle wishes—including, as for most of us, the desire to have a million dollars or to be famous. Although we would be happy to have these things, we place no particular importance on having them. So, we do not work toward having them, ponder our progress toward success, feel disappointed that we have yet to achieve them, and so on.

No doubt all of us have desires of both these kinds. Consider, now, the hopeless desire, the one that plainly has virtually no chance of ever being satisfied. The desire to be a millionaire might be like that, or to be a movie star—or to be someone with whom a particular actress is utterly smitten. There is nothing dubious about having such desires, it seems to me, as long as they remain more or less idle wishes. They are then the stuff of daydreams and fantasies.

What can be troubling, though, is for an adult to take such a desire very seriously, placing great importance upon satisfying it. "Grow up," we might want to say. "Be realistic— stop wasting your time." The charge is childishness, that is. The adult is engaging in something that we indulge in very young adolescents, partly because we do not expect them to be at all clear about what their limits are and partly because nothing is lost by their being unrealistic for a while yet. When we criticize hopeless desire in an adult, we do so partly because we see costs in his refusal to treat it as an idle wish. We also do so partly because we expect him to have learned enough to know that some things are beyond him, and to be mature enough to accept this by (at least) reducing them to the status of daydreams.

Now, to be thoroughly jealous of those who have something we lack is a way of placing importance upon having this thing. Were it only an idle wish, its being given to another would not be upsetting or would be only momentarily so. So the person who burns with jealousy shows thereby that for him it is no idle wish that has gone unsatisfied. His jealousy can be childish, then, not because it is childish to want the thing in question, but because it is childish to place great importance upon having it. Jealousy of the movie actress's male friends is childish in this way, it seems to me.

There is also a sense in which childish jealousy involves overreaching oneself. To be jealous of the movie star's boyfriend is to act as if she were not utterly unattainable by the likes of me; not the stuff of daydreams, but someone whom I have a reasonable chance of attracting. Since I obviously do not, this is to overestimate myself and my prospects. Humility, I have claimed, consists in knowing oneself well enough to be disinclined to overestimation. If so, a humble person would be unlikely to have the kind of jealousy that derives from taking unobtainable desires seriously. He or she might have such desires—don't we all have some?—but the self-knowledge in humility would keep them in the category of idle wishes.

That might seem a small relief, at best. Surely *you* do not yearn for any movie stars, in this curiously earnest way? So, since you are scarcely vulnerable to this kind of jealousy anyway, the fact that humility would protect you from it does not seem much of a recommendation. But how certain can you be that you are not similarly foolish in any of your other cherished hopes? You take those hopes seriously, and therefore you certainly do not recognize that they are unattainable. But this does not bring them within your reasonable prospects.

Moreover, hopeless desires are especially likely to engender jealousy toward those who succeed where we fail, since here we do not have those little successes of our own that make it easier to take another's flourishing in stride. For example, if you are often considered a person of intelligence, it may be relatively easy to accept someone else being given this same regard. By contrast, if no one ever thinks you are bright, and this is something you badly want, those same admiring comments about his cleverness may be much harder to accept. In sum, there may well be more hopeless desires among our fondest hopes than we realize, and such desires are likely to engender jealousy. If humility does provide an obstacle to this, that is not so small a thing as it might at first appear.

4

Thus far the topic has been jealousy of the kind we call childish, or unreasonable, or even "insane." I have argued that the self-knowledge involved in humility would protect a person from jealousy of this kind. We also sometimes tell people that they "have a *right* to be jealous," however. What do we mean by this? Does humility bear in some way on feeling jealous when one has a right to?

The first point to be made is that to say someone has a right to be jealous does not mean merely that she is correct in thinking that the object of her affections now favors another. That much would be true of the man who is jealous of the movie star's lovers, or of his wife's friends, and surely such people do not have any right to be jealous. We seem to mean instead that the jealous person is entitled not to be treated as he has been. He did have a commitment—or, at least, ample encouragement to think he had one—and that commitment is now being broken. Thus the people we support by saying "You have a right to be jealous" are not the ones who merely hanker after someone who has given them no encouragement and are now bitter because their dreams have not come true. The people we support by saying they have a right to be jealous are the husbands and wives, the steady girlfriends and boyfriends.

However, although we certainly do talk in the way described, the whole idea of a right to be jealous is actually very odd. Consider first its role in supporting a man's being jealous of his wife's lover, for example. Suppose that his right to be jealous does derive from his being entitled to think he had a commitment from his wife not to take any lovers. That commitment would have been from his wife, not from the lover. So although her behavior might justify being upset with her, why does it also justify being upset with the man with whom she is sleeping? Why does it give the husband a right to be jealous of the lover, that is, rather than just entitling him to be angry at his wife?

One answer is that we wonder about this only because we picture the wife's lover as entirely passive in all this. Adultery is not something a person does alone, after all. Indeed, the affair might even be more the lover's doing than the wife's: his idea in the first place, his instigation, his steady and skillful persuasion, his soothing of doubts and making of arrangements. She might be guilty mainly of having been willing to be seduced, that is, rather than playing a more active role. Not that this necessarily leaves her blameless: the point is that both parties are probably blameworthy, rather than she alone. They have broken the wife's commitment together, rather than this being something she did by herself; the lover may even have dominated the joint activity. All of this suggests that if the breaking of the commitment justifies the husband in being angry at her, it may well justify his being angry at her lover as well.

I believe it can also be argued that we ought not to allow others to break promises for our sake, if we know them to be promises that ought to be kept. If so, it will not matter if the affair was the wife's project while he was more passive. On this view he would be wrong to play even that part, in the same way someone would be wrong to let a person spend money on him if he knew she was morally obliged to spend it on someone else.

If this view is correct, adulterers wrong cuckolds not only when they actively seduce the cuckold's wife but whenever they know her broken commitment is one that ought to be kept. Not everyone will agree with this view, of course. Moreover, we would have to work out the circumstances under which vows of sexual fidelity would qualify as commitments an outside party knows ought to be kept, before we could know how sweepingly this view condemns adultery. All that can wait for another time, however.

Here the thing to notice is that (like others) this effort to explain how a husband could have a right to be jealous of his wife's lover runs toward showing that the lover did him wrong. That brings out a second, more intransigent oddness in the idea of a right to be jealous. Suppose, for the sake of argument, that the lover *has* mistreated the husband. We might plausibly say that this entitles the husband to resent the lover as one who wronged him, or to be indignant over the fact that he has been done wrong. What is interesting is that those reactions are not jealousy, if we follow the distinctions drawn earlier. When you are jealous, what occasions the hard feelings is not the perception that this person has done you an injustice, or that he has profited from an injustice someone else committed. When you are jealous, you are upset with him over the (perceived) fact that someone else has given him what you wanted that person to give to you. Why would those particular hard feelings be justified?

They are not, after all, hard feelings about having had a commitment violated. They are feelings we have even when we are fully aware that we have *had* no commitment. They derive entirely from wanting to be favored by someone, taking that desire seriously (as opposed to having it as an idle wish), and believing that this other party is favored in our stead.

Our talk of a right to be jealous is confused, I want to suggest. We should be telling such people they have a right to be upset or a right to feel mistreated or betrayed or a right to be angry at this person for initiating their mistreatment (or, on some views, for participating in it), not that they have a right to be jealous. Indeed, although we might plausibly say someone's jealousy was reasonable rather than baseless or childish, it is not easy to see what could ground a right to be jealous: a right, that is, to be upset over the bare fact that this person was favored in a way the jealous person wished to be.

Humility would come into play as follows. If the preceding discussion is sound, a "right to be jealous" is really a right to be angry with someone over a certain kind of mistreatment you have suffered. It obtains when you have a commitment (or, at least, are justified in thinking you have a commitment) from one of the parties to the effect that you will not be treated in this way. It is not always obvious when you have such a commitment: sometimes the commitment is unspoken, and it may also be possible to forfeit a commitment by your own conduct. So, knowing when you have a right to feel mistreated can require a certain sensitivity about your place in the life of another person and about what behavior on your part would violate the relationship and cancel its commitments. Humility would undercut presumptuousness about this, it seems to me: it would help you not to overestimate your position.

To put it a bit differently, it is the person who *lacks* humility who always feels aggrieved when she is not favored: who always feels not just that she has not obtained something she badly wants but that she has been *wronged*, that is. It is she who presumes that things ought to work out her way, perhaps because she is one of nature's elect, and therefore that she always has a right to be jealous. A humble person would know better. She would be better at realizing that she had no right to be indignant.

I am not claiming here that humility ensures that we are jealous only when we have a right to be (only when we have a right to be indignant, that is). To be jealous we need only yearn to be special to someone, believe those yearnings to be disappointed, and react with negative feelings toward the lucky party. We need not take ourselves to be entitled to that for which we yearn, and so any special sensitivity about our entitlements is irrelevant. Humility does, however, provide a basis for keeping our yearnings reasonable and probably also for recognizing when it is our own fault that these reasonable yearnings have not been satisfied rather than this being something we can hold against someone else. It may thereby reduce the occasions for jealousy.

Even reasonable desires are sometimes disappointed, however. Nor can humility alone ensure that one's reaction to disappointment will be reasonable. So, humility cannot quite make us invulnerable to jealousy, only safe from it insofar as it stems from desperate insecurity or from childishness or from an exaggerated sense of when we have a right to some hard feelings.

Now to consider the relation of humility to envy.

5

Earlier, I suggested that to be envious is to believe that a certain individual has had some accomplishment that you have not or has had a piece of good luck that has not befallen you or has some sterling characteristic that you lack, and to have this perception affect negatively your feelings about that person. It is interesting to note that not every perceived disparity makes us envious: it is perfectly possible to recognize that you have been surpassed without being the least bit upset about it. In fact, anyone with any sense must recognize that he or she has innumerable betters in most if not all dimensions. Yet, scarcely anyone is steadily asmolder with envy. Why is it that some disparities spark envy, while others leave us indifferent or even arouse admiration for the person who has done so well?

When we are indifferent, it seems to me, it is often because we place no importance on the respect in which we have been surpassed. For example, if your neighbor has a far better automobile than you do, this may make your son envy his son, while leaving you quite unstirred. The difference can be just that your son cares greatly about the state of "his" automobile, while this matters very little to you. The same can hold for personal qualities and for accomplishments. Perhaps your neighbor has more charm and a wonderful front lawn, but this fails to make you envious because you simply do not care very much about these particular things.

Humility is relevant to this situation only insofar as it bears on which things matter to a person. Humility *does* bear on that, it seems to me, in the way noted in connection with unreasonable jealousy. That is, humility helps to keep a person's aspirations within the realm of the sensible. Knowing yourself means knowing what is beyond a person like you, and this prevents your placing great importance on the unobtainable through simple ignorance of its being unobtainable. That eliminates some kinds of envy, including the kind that regularly edges into railing against the injustice of a life in which you are not doing as well as someone of (what you believe to be) your abilities and qualities deserves to do.

Consider, though, the case in which a person does care appreciably about the respect in which she has been surpassed but is still able to take the matter in stride rather than becoming bitter toward the one who has outdone her. Some of those who manage this seem simply to have an abundance of self-confidence. It appears that a single defeat does not bother them because they have no serious doubts about themselves. Since being surpassed confirms no dark suspicions lurking in their souls, they have no need to be angry at those who confirm such suspicions by surpassing them.

Humility would help us attain this perspective, insofar as an accurate understanding of ourselves would reveal a wide range of things with which to be pleased. For many of us it would do exactly that, I believe. But even for those it did so serve, having a good sense of themselves would not ensure that they would be reasonable in what they demanded of themselves. It is possible to be quite a capable and accomplished person, to understand your capacities and acomplishments, and still to be very disappointed in yourself. Hence humility is consistent with lacking the broad self-approval that enables some to take disappointments so gracefully. It cannot insure this kind of disinclination to envy, because it is not identical with self-approval or with reasonability in the demands one makes of oneself.

Consider next Thomas Aquinas's very different idea about why we are only sometimes envious when others outstrip us. Aquinas held that we envy only those with whom we

take ourselves to be in competition, and that we sensibly restrict the field of our competitors to those who are more or
less like us.

> A man is envious of those only whom he wishes to
> rival or surpass in reputation. But this does not ap-
> ply to people who are far removed from one an-
> other: for no man, unless he be out of his mind,
> endeavors to rival or surpass in reputation those
> who are far above him. Thus a commoner does not
> envy the king . . . Wherefore a man envies not those
> who are far removed from him, whether in place,
> time, or station, but those who are near him, and
> whom he strives to rival or surpass.[15]

Those who are not like us we are free to admire or to
ignore, on this view. We can feel that what has happened has
nothing in particular to do with us, rather than feeling that we
have been beaten at something by someone we should be able
to surpass.

Aquinas was certainly right to think of envy as a competitive emotion, a feeling of distress over having been surpassed.
If the trick to avoiding it is to cease considering ourselves to
be in competition, however, it seems that envy will be particularly difficult for Americans to avoid. We revere competition,
and we admire the ambition to compete against the very best.
Our economic system is based on competition and we love
sports. We love chanting "We're number one," and we accept
statements such as "Winning may not be the only thing, but
it's way ahead of whatever is in second place," and "Show me
a good loser and I'll show you a loser." When we hear that our
children have done well in school, we find it natural to ask
how the other kids did. Ostensibly, this is to determine how
difficult our own child's achievement was, but it carries another message as well: what matters is that you did better than

they did; what matters is that you beat them. We aim to win, and we have much self-esteem wrapped up in whether we do win. That is fertile ground for resenting those who beat us, and for regularly worrying about how we are doing in comparison to others. Assuming envy is something we want to avoid, how are we to accomplish this, under such conditions?

The most fundamental maneuver is to manage, somehow, to keep score differently: you against the task, or you against your ideal of yourself, rather than you against the others engaged in that same task. This shift of attitude requires accepting the idea that, although it matters what sort of person you are, it is only your own behavior that can bear on this. Even the fact that someone is a far better human being than you are has nothing to do with how honest or generous you happen to be yourself, how loyal to your friends or reliable under pressure. Your qualities would not differ if this other person were to vanish from the face of the earth or were never to have existed at all. You would still be whatever person you are. Thus, if your interest is in what sort of person you are, any hard feelings toward her for being a better person are beside the point.

Someone who managed this shift of attitude would retain an interest in how others were doing, but only because of the indirect light this shed on her own performance. How others have done—and, more specifically, how they managed to do so very well—can show that, unlike them, you have lacked a certain singleness of purpose, perhaps, or have been a bit lazy or careless. That could justify being disappointed in yourself, of course. But disappointment in yourself is not the same as envy, and this is as far as the feelings would go, if you believed that the sort of person someone else was had no *bearing* on what sort you were.

How one manages to adopt this rational-sounding attitude is something of a mystery. I want to suggest, though, that it has some connections with the realism about oneself that I associate with humility. For, notice how many of the competitions that frame the envious person's life are wholly imaginary. A man knows that his colleague has a wonderful sabbatical arranged, for example, while he must toil away at the same dreary stand, and he is envious. He takes this to be a case of falling behind his colleague—but in truth there is no competition here for who has the best life. Or, again, he hears that someone with whom he went to school is doing exceptionally well, and it makes him envious, as if he were being beaten in a race—but there is no race. Or he envies the town's richest man, as if the difference in their bank accounts would be reflected in a score sheet kept somewhere—but this is an illusion, surely.

These mistaken convictions that you are involved in a competition exaggerate your place in the world, I think. They posit connections where there are none, rather like the paranoia that sees plots against you where there is only indifference. These are ways of taking what happens, not exactly to center on you, but definitely to involve you much more extensively than it actually does. The cold truth is that very little of what happens has anything whatever to do with any given individual: to think otherwise is to overestimate your place in the universe. A more humble perspective is thus a basis for avoiding the envy in which you invent the competition, since humility disinclines you to picture the universe in this way. It would at least permit you to take the noncompetitive, nonenvious attitude where it would have been you who created the competition.

Not all competitions are our own inventions, though. If all the raises are funded from the same limited pool, your colleague's accomplishments do put you behind. If you envy her for them, you are not (unhumbly) imagining some connection between her fortunes and yours: there really is one. Similarly, there are sales contests within a company, Olympic teams to be made, and world records to be sought. Some competitions are not imaginary, and other competitors do sometimes surge ahead in them. How is one to avoid envy here, and what (if anything) has humility got to do with doing so?

Cicero once suggested that it would not be envy a person felt on such occasions but something else, which he called "rivalry":

> Envy they say is distress incurred by reason of a neighbour's prosperity, though it does no harm to the envious person; for if anyone were to be grieved by the prosperity of one by whom he conceives himself injured, he would not rightly be described as envious, as for instance if Agamemnon were said to envy Hector.[16]

Distinguishing between envy and rivalry does have some appeal. Intuitively, there does seem to be a difference between being upset with someone for beating you at cards or in a foot-race and envying that person. You could *also* envy her the prize she won or be jealous of the attention her victory brought her, of course. The point is that your bitterness toward her for beating you seems to be a different thing.

Along these same lines, one sometimes reads of world-class athletes who are so fiercely competitive that they cannot bear to lose at anything, sulking for hours if they are beaten at a trivial board game or hand of cards. Living with such people sounds pretty unbearable—the term "childish" comes to mind, again—but to call their bitterness toward anyone who beats them envy seems wrong.

Cicero is not much help about how to distinguish such feelings from envy, however. His definition of rivalry is very close to our analysis of envy: "Rivalry is distress, should another be in possession of the object desired and one has to go without it oneself."[17] We might do better by emphasizing the feelings of injury, here, feelings that the winner has done something harmful to the person who lost by beating him. Sometimes it would not be a sense just of injury but of mistreatment: the other person "wasn't supposed to win", "it's not fair" . . .

Both varieties have an element missing from envy, which does not emphasize in this way the role of the person envied as the agent of what upsets me. I can envy someone I see as the passive recipient of good fortune, as long as the difference between our estates makes me angry at her; I can feel injured or wronged by her only insofar as I think of her as having done something to me.

If that is the difference, however, it does not enable us to say that people do not feel envy (but feel only rivalry) when the contest is real. To return to an earlier example, suppose your colleague received a bigger raise from the funds allotted for raises in your department. There was a real competition between the two of you, and you lost. You might be bitter toward her without thinking of her as having injured you, let alone thinking of her as having done you wrong. She won fair and square, blast her, and what upsets you now is the fact that she will be getting a large raise and you will not. You are envious, and since the competition was not something you imagined, we are back to our question: what (if anything) has humility got to do with envying those who really have defeated us in a contest?

There can be at least this much, it seems. A loser's hard feelings can resemble the overreaction of a person who has been harmed. Each takes an event to be somehow momentous, obscuring everything else the other person is or has done. In the eyes of the unhappy party, she is now mainly the person who received the bigger raise, won the tennis match, or whatever. Never mind whatever else she has done or whatever else they have been to each other: her role in this one event becomes central to his conception of her.

It is obvious that this can exaggerate the importance of this event, and thus the importance of his being defeated. It is also obvious that it can be part of treating his being defeated much more seriously than he would consider it appropriate for others to react to similar defeats. An overreaction to a defeat is a failure of humility, in these ways. To put it differently, humility inclines a person not to be a sore loser, since it keeps defeats in a reasonable perspective.

A different way to avoid hard feelings toward those who defeat one would be to avoid being defeated, of course. Not a very plausible strategy, admittedly, but a person might at least be prudent in the competitions he or she chose to enter. Clearly there is a role for humility here, as well: those who lack it will choose the wrong people to compete against and will often have to deal with not having fared as well as they had hoped. The strategies of envy will be available to them to soothe their troubled egos and sustain their illusions, by attributing the defeat to injustice or denigrating the competitor's achievement, or disparaging the competitor himself. Humility can be a bar against the need for such devices, by making one realistic about whom to compete against in the first place.

Still, what about the competitions that cannot be avoided? The competitions, that is, that are thrust upon us rather than being our (perhaps unhumble) choice? Aristotle speaks to these:

> We compete with our rivals in some contest, with our rivals in love—in a word, with those who seek the same things that we seek, so that these persons above all must be the ones whom we envy. And hence the saying (of Hesiod . . .):
>
> And potter 'gainst potter.[18]

Although it may not always be our option whether to enter a competition, however, it is always up to us whether we take the competition to heart. Envy is a sign that we *have* taken it to heart, which is why we can be made upset by the accomplishments of our competitors. Thus, a person's choice of which competitions he takes seriously reflects his self-conception as readily as his choice of which competitions to enter. Here, again, someone who thought too highly of himself would be troubled by the progress of those far more capable than he, rather than being able to take that in stride or to admire it from the outside, as it were. To draw once more on Aristotle: "We envy those whose acquisitions and successful efforts are a reproach to us . . . for it is evidently our own fault that we have missed the 'good' in question, and the subsequent pain makes for envy."[19] For someone who overestimates himself, life will present many such reproaches; for a person of humility, they should be fewer.

It would be a bolder thesis to say that a humble person would never be envious, because such a person would never take any competition seriously or would never think of herself as in competition with others. That would be a bold thesis, but, I think, a false one. It may be, as Immanuel Kant would urge, that nothing anyone else is or does can affect a person's own moral worth. It might even be true that anyone who understood his own worth, as a humble person would, would necessarily grasp this fact about worth. If so, it would follow that humility frees a person from one source of envy. For, certainly, some envy is an effort to cope with sinking feelings that you have not turned out to be much.

Not all envy is of this kind, however. Accordingly, freedom from this kind of envy would not be freedom from envy altogether. For example, if someone wins a lottery, it is possible to envy him because you just badly want what that winning would bring, even though you do not consider yourself a lesser human being for not being that rich or for not having won yourself. Similarly, suppose you are upset about someone's being so much more clever than you, or even about his having done something you had always hoped to do yourself. Certainly, your feelings can include doubts about your moral value—but they need not. Just to have deep yearnings makes you vulnerable to envy toward those whose lives (innocently) remind you that these yearnings are unsatisfied.

As with jealousy, there is nothing in humility that precludes having such yearnings or that guarantees a mature reaction when they are disappointed. So, humility precludes neither envy nor jealousy. On the other hand, it does stand in the way of envy in which one imagines a competition that does not exist, and it can help reduce the envy that arises from being exceeded by those to whom it is unreasonable to compare oneself. It is also proof against jealousy without cause and the all-encompassing jealousy that besets those we call "insanely" jealous. In short, humility tends to limit envy and jealousy to situations in which feeling envy or jealousy is reasonable; it helps protect us from having such feelings when they would be unreasonable.

5

PATERNALISM
AND
ARROGANCE

For many of us, the sight of someone who is about to make a mistake produces a powerful urge to intervene. The mistake this person is about to make need not be an especially costly one. If it simply appears that she will be doing less well than she could, that can be enough to make us want to step forward. In this respect, the urge to prevent mistakes is unlike compassion, which is aroused only when we think that someone is in grave distress: here, something much less dramatic can be sufficient.

There is a second difference: compassion always involves concern for the individual whom one believes to be in trouble. The urge to prevent a mistake can be like that, but it can also be entirely impersonal. It can be a feeling that the proceedings are about to be marred, as if by a misstep in a march, so that the shudder at what is happening is less sympathetic than aesthetic. Those inclined to such shudders do not intervene to protect the person who is about to blunder. Their motivation is to prevent error, not to protect individuals; they intervene because (as they see things) a mistake will be made if they do not.

Probably some of what is usually called paternalism is perfectionism of this sort. Although we say we are intervening for this person's "own good" on such occasions, actually we have no concern for him at all. What moves us is the more abstract desire that the right thing be done, rather than the wrong one on which he seems to have fastened.

Imagine, for example, that our colleague habitually bolts his food, eating so voraciously that adults are inclined to don their raincoats and to shield the eyes of their children from the sight. This behavior brings our colleague indigestion, high cleaning bills, and considerable ostracism as an uncivilized boor. Although correcting someone's table manners is a delicate matter, we resolve to press him to change his ways: for his own good, we hasten to say, and that may be the truth. But it can also be that we would want him to change even if he were totally indifferent to these costs himself, or if we did not care about his suffering them. It can be, that is, that we just think this is *no way to eat*.

For a second example, think of the physician who wants to ensure that her patient follows a particular regimen. The patient's gall bladder should be removed, she urges, not left untreated and not treated with medications, and the physician uses every tactic she can to enforce this choice. All for his own good, of course, because she cares about him? Perhaps; but it can also be that she is simply convinced that surgery is the proper solution to this particular medical puzzle. She wants the gall bladder removed because, in her professional judgment, that is the right thing to do in a case like this, and she would want it removed even if she had no interest at all in this particular man.

When the urge to prevent a mistake is perfectionist in this way, it is unlike compassion in its focus. The difference is not that compassionate people are emotional while perfectionists are cold fish: there can be a great deal of emotion in perfectionism. The difference is that the compassionate person's concern is for the individual, while the perfectionist's concern (and emotion) is that things be done (as he thinks) properly.

Efforts to prevent mistakes from being made can have either focus. Indeed, paternalism can have either focus, if we follow those who explain paternalism as "the sort of concern a father would have for his children." For, although certainly fathers do help their children out of affection, sometimes, at other times they are perfectionists, and at still others they have both motivations. To avoid this ambiguity, suppose we think of paternalism as motivated always by concern for the individual one seeks to correct, and perfectionism as the less personal behavior.

Consider, then, the genuinely paternalistic urge to intervene, motivated by concern for the person who is about to go wrong. Here is genuine good will for a fellow creature, an urgent wish that things should go better for him than they are about to. As noted, the wish is not just that he should not be utterly miserable, as when we have compassion for someone. The wish is that he should do better even in small ways: essentially, that he should do as well as it is possible for him to do.

That might seem beyond reproach, as an attitude toward a fellow human being. It is part of what we want from our friends, when we want them to care about us. "You could see what I was about to do," we might say to a friend; "how could you stand by and let me do it? I thought we were friends . . ."

Notoriously, however, this is also the attitude that leads to the most overbearing and intrusive behavior. It is possible to be oversolicitous, that is, and even though the oversolicitous person's behavior might be loving, or at least personally concerned, we still want it to stop. Defining the difference between concern we ought to appreciate and concern that goes too far is a classic problem, not only of philosophy but of living with people about whom we care. This chapter takes up this problem.

The now standard account of what is wrong with concern that goes too far employs a political metaphor of sovereign territory and inviolable borders. Just as nations have their

boundaries, we are each said to have a "realm of personal autonomy where each competent, responsible adult human being
should reign supreme."[1] On this account, some paternalism violates our personal boundaries, just as one nation might violate
the boundaries of another—though nations usually invade other
nations out of pure self-interest and not out of tender concern for
those they invade. But perhaps that disanalogy is less jarring, in
a time when political rhetoric speaks of fighting "wars of libera-
tion," of "spreading the revolution," and (at least until recently)
of "freeing the poor _____ from the yoke of Communism."

At any rate, this talk of realms of autonomy is the model
of our time for thinking about paternalism, and it is very rich.
Here I want neither to challenge it nor to deploy it. I try instead to develop a slightly different idea: namely, that there is
arrogance in some efforts to help people, whether those efforts
be sympathetic or perfectionist. I think it is arrogance we are
complaining about when an especially heavy-handed effort to
ensure that someone acts "in his own best interest" prompts
us to mutter, "Who does she think she is?" or "What makes
her think this is up to her?" We are thinking that the paternalist has too high an opinion of herself, or too low an opinion of
the person she thinks she must help. We need to consider that
reaction more closely, to see when we are right to think of
such behavior as arrogant and what makes it so.

That will be of help in the larger project of saying what it
would be to live with humility, for surely arrogance and humility are antithetical. Insofar as a measure is arrogant, that
should put a humble person off, more strongly the clearer the
arrogance and the deeper his humility. What does this imply,
for a humble person who encounters someone who seems
about to make a mistake? The idea is to try to say. The first
step is to consider the nature of arrogance.

1

Imagine that you are in your neighborhood bakery on a Sunday morning, part of a considerable crowd seeking breakfast

pastries. Suddenly, the mayor's teenaged son enters. He walks straight through the waiting customers to the nearest clerk and announces his order. He expects to be served immediately because he is the mayor's son.[2]

This behavior is highly annoying. What is annoying about it is that it seems so arrogant. The boy apparently believes that being the mayor's son makes him better than everyone else, puts him above those who must wait their turn. If that is what he thinks, his error is not in taking himself to be the mayor's son but in exaggerating the importance of his position. He takes it to carry certain entitlements that it simply does not, and he has no adequate reason to construe it as he does.

As another illustration, think of Lord Nelson, who apparently believed that his accomplishments as an admiral entitled him to do virtually anything he wished. He was encouraged in this by public adulation, but it was still arrogant of him to assume, for example, that prevailing at the Battle of the Nile entitled him to the wife of the ambassador to Naples.[3] As with the mayor's son, Lord Nelson leapt to a certain rather startling conclusion about something that was true of him: he had won the battle, just as the boy was the mayor's son.

It is possible to be arrogant in a different way: not in what you take your qualities to entail, but in what qualities you take yourself to have. For example, it is probably right to suppose that someone who knows a great deal more about the subject under discussion than most of those present is entitled to have her opinions taken with some seriousness. That supposition does not overestimate this quality, unlike, for example, supposing that your opinions should be taken seriously because you are the mayor's son. Still, there could be arrogance here, in your thinking that you do know more about the subject than most of those present. The arrogance would consist in believing this without adequate justification, I want to suggest.

Of course, unjustified beliefs tend also to be false, generally speaking, and the same is true here. The mayor's son is not only unjustified but also mistaken, when he thinks that his father's position entitles him to receive first service in the bakery or to have his ideas on all subjects considered worthy of careful consideration. Lord Nelson is wrong about his entitlements, as well. Still, it is their epistemic presumptuousness that makes these beliefs arrogant, I argue, not their being mistaken.

To see this, let us vary our examples a bit. Imagine first a mayor's son who is correct about being entitled to go to the head of the line, but not at all for the reasons he thinks that he is. By sheerest chance, he is the bakery's ten thousandth customer, and this entitles him not only to jump the queue but, indeed, to have his purchases free of charge. That entitlement is entirely unknown to him and does not figure in his thinking, however. When he swaggers forward to demand these things, it is wholly on the basis of his being the mayor's son, as before; and, as before, there is not a shred of evidence that being the mayor's son glorifies him in the way he takes it to.

His behavior is just as arrogant as it was in the simpler case, it seems to me. The fact that he is accidentally correct about his entitlements is irrelevant. If so, a person can be right about his entitlements and still be arrogant in thinking he has them. This indicates that arrogance does not consist in being wrong about your entitlements but consists in something else.

Moreover, it is also possible to be wrong about your entitlements without being arrogant. If so, again, arrogance does not consist in being mistaken but consists in the kind of mistake you make. As an illustration, imagine that a friend tells you the group in the corner are enthusiastic beginners at baking breads and desserts, eager to learn all they can but with very little experience. He urges you to share your expertise with them. You think you do have something to offer, for you have done this sort of baking for years, with considerable success. As you approach them you hear "Puff pastry . . ." and see a general shaking of heads. You modestly offer a basic tip or two. To your astonishment, one of the group actually laughs, and several others seem to exchange sardonic smiles.

Your friend is usually very reliable, but this time he is horribly wrong. These are not amateurs: they are professional chefs, and, worse yet, specialists in fine desserts. Have you been arrogant, in believing that you knew more about the subject than the others and therefore expecting your opinions to be taken seriously? That would be too harsh a judgment, it seems to me. You had excellent reason to think you had something to offer, even though you were mistaken. The message, again, is that arrogance does not consist in being mistaken about your position but consists in leaping to a favorable opinion about it (or, where this is too athletic a picture, in maintaining such an opinion despite the overwhelming evidence against it).

There is an objection to this analysis that helps to set it out more fully. The objection begins with the observation that at least some of those who act arrogantly are encouraged to do so by the overblown esteem of others. Consider again Lord Nelson, madly cheered by his entire nation. The objection is that this adulation provided him grounds for believing what all about him were saying: namely, that he was a godlike figure, entitled to act exactly as he chose. He had justification aplenty; so, the objection continues, he did not act arrogantly after all, on the suggested analysis. But surely he did—and so the analysis must be mistaken.

Notice, however, that although Nelson had some basis for believing that he was godlike, he had only about enough to move this belief out of the class of the lunatic. We can readily understand how he could have come to believe himself godlike, that is, because we know he was encouraged to believe it was true. But despite our understanding, the crowd's adulation did not also make this something it was *reasonable* for Nelson to believe. For one thing, there was no reason for him to think that cheering crowds are good judges of whether one is a creature to whom ordinary strictures do not apply. For another, he should have regarded this hypothesis with considerable suspicion: it has a great deal against it from the outset.

Compare here the baker who accepted a picture of himself as knowing more about pastry than the other conversants. He was told as much, not by an ignorant crowd, but by someone he could expect to be telling the truth. And, given his years of successful baking, the idea had some initial plausibility. Nelson and the baker both accept welcome pictures of themselves, but only Nelson is unreasonable to do so; and so only Nelson is arrogant.

In short, Nelson was arrogant because he lacked sufficient justification to make his belief a reasonable one, not because he had no reason for it at all. Roughly speaking, arrogance is exaggeration, not invention: *sheer* invention is madness. Arrogance, like justification, comes in degrees. The closer a person's evidence comes to justifying her belief, the less arrogant she is in adopting it; the greater the leap, the greater the arrogance.

That is why there is a foolishness to some high arrogance that is almost amusing, as when the distinguished political theorist, for example, takes it for granted that he is the one who must organize the departmental picnic. Chaos ensues, but he carries on, wondering only why it is that these people cannot carry out his plans—perhaps they are just shockingly poor stock? Even this behavior is not utterly baseless, of course, for the distinguished political theorist has good reason to think of himself as an intelligent, capable person. It is just that his confidence is broader and stronger than it should be.

Why would a person make the kind of mistake that arrogant people make? The question is especially intriguing in that arrogance sometimes afflicts very intelligent people. Precious few of their other beliefs are unreasonable: why these? One generous view is that arrogant people make these leaps out of desperation, out of fear that they may not be wonderful people after all. On this account, in their hearts they suspect that an accurate picture of themselves would be pretty appalling, and so they never look closely.

Perhaps this is the truth about some arrogant people; perhaps we should try to be at least somewhat sympathetic toward the arrogant rather than being automatically annoyed by them. As a generalization, though, it would probably be overgenerous. For, there are other reasons not to be careful about a subject than fear of what one might find. It may be that Sebastian does not think carefully about himself because he is confident that he already knows the wonderful answer, not because he is afraid of what the answer might be. It may be that Miranda does not think carefully about herself because she does not think carefully about anything; she believes her intelligence is too penetrating to require her to take care. If so, what underlies Sebastian's and Miranda's arrogance is not a lack of self-esteem but more arrogance. And, of course, the reason they are arrogant at this deeper level need not be a still deeper lack of self-esteem: some arrogant people just seem to be arrogant through and through.

Sebastian, Miranda, Lord Nelson, and the mayor's son all exemplify arrogance of the sort in which someone believes himself or herself entitled to act and to be treated in certain ways. There is also arrogance of another kind: there are individuals who simply do not consider the question whether they are entitled to act as they do to be one of any importance. They care whether the course of action interests them but not how it affects others or whether it is "within their rights," or whether it is right or wrong. They take license in a way that is certainly arrogant, but one that differs from the way Lord Nelson and the mayor's boy do.

As an illustration, consider the following exchange from Henry James's The Portrait of a Lady. The first speaker is Madame Merle, who proposes to bring together the naive heroine and the man to whom she is speaking, for purposes she conceals from both parties.

> "She's beautiful, accomplished, generous, and, for an American, well-born. She's also very clever and very amiable, and she has a handsome fortune."
>
> Mr. Osmond listened to this in silence, appearing to turn it over in his mind with his eyes on his informant. "What do you want to do with her?" he asked at last.
>
> "What you see. Put her in your way."
>
> "Isn't she meant for something better than that?"
>
> "I don't pretend to know what people are meant for," said Madame Merle. "I only know what I can do with them."[4]

Merle's sole concern is what she can "do with" the heroine, how she can use her for her own purposes. She makes no claim to be entitled to act as she does—unlike, say, some zealous matchmaker relying vaguely on "knowing what's best" for the young woman or on superior wisdom about the ways of the world. Merle is not overestimating her entitlements and going a bit too far: she is wholly uninterested in such matters. She simply does not think in those terms, and if she were forced to acknowledge that she had no right to act as she did, she would regard this as irrelevant.

In short, Merle puts herself above morality; there is arrogance in that, surely, no less than there is arrogance in certain presumptuous beliefs that one is acting perfectly appropriately because one is special in some way. Of course, Merle is not acting paternalistically, and the arrogance in some paternalism is our underlying interest in this chapter, but it is easy enough to imagine a paternalist with Merle's sort of unconcern for the morality of his behavior. "I don't care about that," a father with such an attitude might say. "All I care about is our daughter's welfare. I am not going to let her make a terrible mistake and ruin her life. I will prevent that in any way I can, and if that means going beyond my rights then so be it."

This father is unlike Madame Merle in one interesting way. What he considers more important than right and wrong is his daughter's welfare. What Merle considers more important than the rightness or wrongness of what she does is its effectiveness in serving her personal aims: its capacity to entertain her in a particular way, and its status as an exercise of power. Her behavior is thus self-centered in a way his is not: in that respect Merle's behavior puts *her* above morality, whereas this father's behavior puts his *daughter* above morality. In that respect, Merle is arrogant in a way the father is not.

Despite this dissimilarity, the two are also very much alike in another respect: each takes a great license when acting. Each takes moral considerations not to bind them in what they do, however binding those might be for lesser beings. That is the arrogance of particular interest at the moment, in contrast to the sort exemplified by Lord Nelson and the mayor's boy, who believe themselves entitled to act as they do by some special, elevating feature of theirs. Merle and the father take no interest in whether they are entitled to act as they do. There is a connection between these two kinds of arrogance.

First: behavior itself carries certain suppositions, regardless of the agent's beliefs about it. As Jeffrie Murphy urges, to mistreat someone is to act as if it were right to treat her in this way—hence the importance of her protesting the mistreatment. The broader point is that *whenever* we act, we act as if it were a proper way to behave. That is why our actions are open to moral question: we endorse them in doing them, so we can be asked to justify them. We can be asked why they were legitimate things to do, as we apparently think, since we have done them. If we say, "Oh, I never thought it *was* legitimate," this will hardly be satisfactory: we are on a hook less easily escaped, once we have done a thing.

Sometimes, a person knows, believes, or suspects that it would *not* be legitimate to act in a particular way and refrains for that reason. Madame Merle and the paternalistic father are far from having such scruples. Their behavior does carry the usual implication that they are behaving in a legitimate way. They also have excellent grounds for supposing that they are not. They go ahead anyway. Their arrogance consists in this cavalier disregard for the implications of what they do.

In a like manner, the behavior of Lord Nelson and the behavior of the mayor's boy carry the implication that these are legitimate ways for them to behave. And they too have excellent grounds for supposing that their behavior is not legitimate. That is enough to make it arrogant for them to go ahead: as with Merle and the father, their arrogance consists in their behaving in ways they ought to see as beyond their entitlements.

Of course, whether they ought to see this as beyond their entitlements is not a matter of whether they do see it that way. It depends, not on what they happen to believe, but on what it would be reasonable for them to believe. Thus, a person may be perfectly aware that the reasonable view is that he is going too far but he simply does not care, as with Merle and the father, or he may be unaware that he is going too far because he misconceives himself as specially entitled, as with Nelson and the boy. There is arrogance of both kinds.

One final point is that arrogance is a moral fault. This means it can be attributed only to those who qualify as morally responsible for the behavior that prompts us to criticize them. Only then can we say that they ought to see themselves as overstepping their entitlements. Thus, a very small child is not arrogant when she believes wonderful things about herself without adequate justification, because she does not know any better than to make such a mistake and, indeed, cannot know any better. She does not yet have the mental equipment for her ignorance to be culpable. So, it is wrong to criticize her for it morally. We would be doing that if we were to call her arrogant.

The same holds for the mentally incompetent and for the very stupid. Insofar as they are not to blame for the mistakes they make, there is no arrogance in their making them, as there would be if these were the mistakes of a competent person. Accordingly, the illustrations offered here should be taken to feature competent adults, who should know better than to err as they do.

In sum: the arrogance of interest consists in a competent person's acting in a way that would be unreasonable for this person to believe himself or herself entitled to act. Because that belief would be unjustified, in general it would also be false, and the arrogant person would not, in fact, be entitled to act in the way in question. Arrogance is greater the more unjustified the belief would be: the more presumptuous the assumption, the more arrogant one would be to make it.

2

Humility and arrogance are antithetical. That seems straightforward. Now to work out something more specific about what it means.

As a start, surely it is impossible to be both an arrogant person and a humble one. Typically, an arrogant person takes herself to be superior to others and therefore to have certain entitlements that they lack, or to be beyond concern with entitlements in a way others are not. This is part of her continuing picture of herself: typically, then, the presumed superiority is in something permanent or at least relatively stable. It is in her breeding, perhaps, or her education, her intelligence, her accomplishments. Crucially, some if not all of the arrogant person's beliefs are epistemically unsound. She lacks adequate evidence for thinking herself superior in this regard, or for thinking the superiority empowers or privileges her in quite the way she assumes, or both.

By contrast, a humble person is one who has herself pretty much in perspective. She understands who she is and what she has accomplished sufficiently clearly to resist temptations to exaggeration. That clarity works against the leap of self-aggrandizement that shapes the arrogant person's life. A humble person simply knows too much to have in her understanding of herself the kind of sustained carelessness that is the essence of the arrogant personality.

Arrogance is not just a character trait, however: there are also particular acts of arrogance. These need not be performed only by arrogant people; they can also be done by those who are not so set in this way that we could fairly consider arrogance a part of their character. What has humility got to do with particular acts of arrogance?

It seems plausible to say that an act of arrogance would repel a person of humility, in the same way as an act of cruelty would repel a kind person. It is not just that the behavior would not be this person's natural course, would not be the kind of thing he would do as a matter of routine. That much would hold for the multitudes who are neither arrogant nor humble, neither cruel nor kind. Instead, the arrogance or the cruelty is the reverse of this person's natural bent. When others act in these alien ways it may distress him, or it may mostly puzzle him: "How can people do such things?" "What can the attraction be?" As for himself, normally the arrogant or cruel course would not occur to him as an option. If it did (or were it suggested by someone else), he would be strongly inclined against it: for him to choose it, there would have to be (at least) very good reasons why this was the best available option even so. In some instances it might still be impossible for him to bring himself to do it. Finally, were a humble person to act in a way he considered arrogant or a kind one to act in a way she considered cruel, that would be an occasion for later regret, remorse, or even for personal disintegration, depending on the details.

One obvious variable is how plain it is that the behavior would be arrogant. We might expect a humble person to have a relatively good eye for this sort of thing (although not to be omniscient). For, to be clear about what you are like and about the value of your qualities should enable you to see through most bad arguments about these things. Moreover, in understanding your own qualities, you would also have some understanding of related qualities, the ones you knew you did not quite have. That would equip you to recognize a wide range of pretension for what it was.

Those are reasons for expecting that a humble person would be relatively perceptive about which actions would be arrogant for her to take. A different reason is that many such actions proceed on assumptions that are not only unjustified but also false. Since humility involves accuracy about oneself, it protects against making mistakes about one's capacities, for example. Not perfectly, of course; for one thing, honest mistakes are still possible. Still, where the picture is not only false but also unjustified, knowing that it is false would protect one from ignoring the weakness of the grounds and accepting it. Hence, there is another good reason to expect a humble person very often to know arrogance for what it is.

Once a humble person saw something as arrogant, he would be more strongly repelled the greater its arrogance. By saying he would be more strongly repelled, I mean that if others were to do it he would be more deeply distressed or more greatly puzzled, that if it were proposed to him he would need better reasons to overcome his initial aversion, and that the costs to his retrospective peace of mind would be greater. But what exactly is it for one course of action to be more arrogant than another and therefore more repellent to a person of humility?

In arrogance, there is an unjustified belief that one has certain entitlements (or, that moral considerations do not bind one). The more egregious the mistake being made, the greater the arrogance exhibited in making it. This is partly a matter of how thoroughly unjustified the arrogant person's beliefs are. In part, it is also a matter of the strength of his unjustified confidence in himself, the certainty he has that he is, indeed, someone of a special kind. The greater the disparity between the confidence he has in himself and his grounds for that confidence, the worse the mistake he makes, and the more arrogant he is in making it.

Roughly speaking, a humble person will be more strongly put off by a course of action the more blatant its arrogance is in this way. Accordingly, if a humble person were forced to choose between two seemingly arrogant courses, we should expect his humility to incline him toward the less arrogant course as, in his view, the lesser of the two evils.

None of this amounts to saying that a humble person would never act arrogantly, or to overlooking the fact that humility comes in degrees and, therefore, so also does the reaction against arrogant behavior. It does support several other conclusions, however: that a humble person could not also be an arrogant one; that arrogant courses of action would repel a humble person in the same way as cruel behavior would repel a kind one; that the repulsion would be greater the more arrogant the behavior; and that a humble person forced to choose would prefer the less arrogant course to the more arrogant one. Now to see what follows about the relationship between humility and acts of paternalism and perfectionism.

3

Paternalism and perfectionism have in common a quality of interrupting the behavior of others, of steering other people in the direction one thinks they should go. To determine

whether there is arrogance in the assumption that one is entitled to do this, we must determine the basis for making that
assumption. As with the earlier examples, the arrogance can
take either of two forms.

In the first form of arrogance, the person who intervenes
does have the qualities that she takes to entitle her to act as
she does. She is unjustified, however, in thinking these qualities carry that entitlement. Like the boy who thinks being the
mayor's son entitles him to special treatment, she may think,
for example, that being younger than the person she means to
help entitles her to ensure that this person acts as she sees
fit. It is not that she is wrong about being younger, of course; it
is just that there is no justification for believing that being
younger entitles one to exercise such control. So this is arrogance of the same kind that the mayor's boy and Lord Nelson
exhibit.

In the second sort of arrogance, the qualities would carry
the entitlements the person takes them to carry, if only she
had them. Her arrogance is in thinking that she does have
these qualities, as when someone just takes it for granted that
he knows more than anyone else about whatever subject is
under discussion, or that he should be in charge of whatever
project is undertaken. Paternalism that was presumptuous in
this way would be arrogant, as would any sort of taking charge
or overruling of the ideas of others on this same imperious
basis. The fact that the paternalist has genuine affection for
those he thinks he must take in hand and only wants to make
things go well for them does not lessen the arrogance in his
doing so. The presumption of superiority remains, and its lack
of justification still makes the behavior arrogant.

Consider next intelligence, a quality about which it is
certainly possible to be arrogant. It is not at all uncommon for
highly intelligent people to think themselves entitled—indeed, obliged   to look after those who are less intelligent than
they. Evidently, they take their greater intelligence to mean

that they will be better at choosing the course in the other party's best interest than she would be herself. This may be true, when both parties have the same information to which to apply their differing intelligence, or when the more intelligent person's disadvantage in information is not very substantial. Having sometimes found himself in such positions, the more intelligent person might erroneously generalize. He might take it that things would almost always go better if he were to steer, because he is the more intelligent party.

It is easy to imagine versions of this story in which the generalization would not be adequately justified and thus would be a case of arrogance. Perhaps the very bright Sylvia has only rarely improved the less bright Bruno's fortunes or has failed at least as often as she has succeeded or is now faced with a far different kind of situation than those in which she did well in the past or should recognize that this time she simply does not know enough to make a recommendation. If she sweeps on undeterred on such occasions, she will be acting arrogantly, secure in her unjustified belief that being brighter than Bruno means she should control his behavior for his own good.

Sylvia's arrogance might involve mistaking her intelligence for a spooky prescience, thinking of herself as someone who can see the future. Or it might involve overestimating the power of intelligence, thinking that greater intelligence is bound to make one the better judge on any occasion, regardless of any differences in informedness or emotional state. These are ways in which an intelligent person can believe she has a quality she does not, by overestimating a quality she does have. Insofar as the belief is unjustified, they are ways in which to be arrogant about one's intelligence: an arrogance displayed here in acts of paternalism or perfectionism.

Something similar applies to mistaking specialized knowledge for a broader wisdom. Scholarly eminence has been known to turn the scholar's head, imparting a conviction that he or she can speak with authority not only about microbes or astronomy but also about politics or about whether George is right for Cynthia. There is nothing wrong with being interested in something outside one's specialty, but there is something wrong with assuming that expertise in the specialty transfers automatically, making one wise in whatever matter is at hand.

Something very like this also happens when physicians take themselves to be experts about which course is in the patient's best interest. They may be experts about the medical questions, and certainly they are typically more expert about those than the patient. Which course would be in the patient's best interest is a much broader matter, however, and it is arrogant for a doctor to assume that knowing best about the medical questions means he or she also knows best about what the patient should do.

As noted earlier, if there is arrogance in steering someone's actions on the ground that you are brighter, or eminent in your field, or (after all) a physician, then such behavior would repel a person of humility. It could easily be part of a broadly arrogant personality and therefore utterly foreign to the humble person. Even as an occasional temptation, it would put this person off. It would do so more strongly the greater its arrogance: that is, the weaker the basis for thinking that your intelligence (eminence, medical degree) ensured that the outcome would be better if you intervened.

Thus far, however, the arrogance considered has consisted in believing (without adequate justification) that one's intelligence or expertise is a quality that enables one to make things go better on this occasion. We need now to consider whether it is also arrogant to assume that this ability to produce better results, if one had it, would entitle one to intrude. We need to consider, that is, whether assuming this is like jumping the queue because you are the mayor's son: whether it is not only arrogant to think that you have this quality but also arrogant to think the quality carries those entitlements. That is important, since it indicates whether paternalism and perfectionism would put a humble person off even when he was quite justified to think he would improve matters if he intervened or only when he was not justified to think he would improve them.

Whether the ability to improve the results entitles you to decide what is done is a point of great contention in philosophy. Those who want to defend a realm of personal autonomy against paternalism argue strenuously that it does not. Ironically, when John Stuart Mill set out what he regarded as "the strongest of all the arguments" against paternalism, he made the opposite assumption. He assumed that the ability to produce better results does make you the proper decision-maker: his thought was just that other parties were very rarely in this position.[5]

Fortunately, we need not settle this extremely vexed question, for our purposes. For, whether it is arrogant to act on the basis that you can improve the results by doing so is not a matter of whether that ability actually would entitle you to act. Whether it is arrogant depends instead on whether, if it were a mistake to do this, it would be a mistake you ought to know better than to make. Arrogance, as I argued earlier, does not consist in being wrong about your entitlements, but it consists in acting in ways you would not be justified in *believing* yourself entitled to act. It consists in acting in ways it would be unreasonable to consider legitimate. And it is also possible to be wrong about such matters through no fault of your own. Imagine a diplomat newly appointed to a court with an intricate etiquette. Her sense of what she is entitled to do might include some innocent blunders. Those mistakes would not be arrogant, so long as she had taken care and reached reasonable conclusions.

I am inclined to think the same of the belief that being able to make matters go better entitles one to steer another's behavior. If this is a mistake, that is, it is not so obvious a mistake that we should charge those who hold it with arrogance. It is not as if they believed being older entitles them, in itself, to guide someone's life, or that being younger or being male does so. These other beliefs so clearly lack justification that to act on them is, simply, to presume. By contrast, to think you should intervene because (in fact) you could help someone avoid making a serious mistake is not in the same category: at worst, it is more like putting forward a wrong foot in complicated court etiquette.

If so, then when there is arrogance in intervening because you think you can make matters go better, the arrogance is in taking yourself to be in that position. It is in thinking you can improve matters just because (after all) you are much brighter, for example, or because you are older and therefore wiser or younger and therefore clearer headed. Accordingly, a humble person will not necessarily be repelled by all interventions taken on the ground that one can be of assistance, only by those in which this evaluation of one's abilities is itself unjustified. If the question is, for example, whether to tell the passing motorist that the bridge is out up ahead, there is nothing in doing so that should make a humble person balk. If the question is whether to tell the woman being browbeaten at the next table that she would be better off dumping her companion, there is.

4

Consider next those occasions on which the question is not so much whether to intervene as whether to do so in one way or in another. There are a great many ways to influence behavior that seems to you to be going wrong: everything from a few quiet words of warning to making it physically impossible for the person to act differently than you think he should. Mill made sharp distinctions among the potential instruments of paternalism, flatly rejecting some and strongly touting others.

> He cannot rightfully be compelled to do or forbear because it will be better for him to do so. . . . These are good reasons for remonstrating with him, or persuading him, or entreating him, but not for compelling him, or visiting him with any evil in case he do otherwise.[6]

Force and threats are out, as implements of paternalistic concern, while "remonstrating . . . persuading . . . entreating" are in. And not only "in," in the sense of being permissible, but our positive duty:

> Human beings owe to each other help to distinguish the better from the worse and encouragement to choose the former and avoid the latter. They should be forever stimulating each other to increased exercise of their highest faculties and aims toward wise instead of foolish, elevating instead of degrading, objects and contemplations.[7]

The question for us is how humility would incline a person toward this arsenal of intrusive measures.

Not in the same way as Mill would have it. For, Mill wants us to be "forever" stimulating each other to higher pursuits with information and verbal arguments—missing no occasion, apparently, to explain how much better it would be for the objects of our concern if they would exercise more, eat differently, read literature instead of trash, and so on. That this kind of hectoring can lack humility perhaps needs no argument.

To get further, notice that not all paternalistic measures are equally coercive. Some of them leave considerable room for the other party to act differently than one thinks he ought.

Simply providing information exerts very little control over what is eventually done: the other person is free to make whatever he likes of it. Pressing an argument is more insistent, an effort to ensure that a particular conclusion is drawn. Misinforming and concealing facts goes still further, confining the intended beneficiary to your picture of the world and making it that much harder for him to choose differently than you think best. Various forms of bullying in argument are also verbal efforts to force a person down your path.

Making a threat exerts a different form of control—how strong the control is no doubt depends on the threat, the person threatened, and the person making the threat. Offering a bribe might be even more controlling, for some personalities. Finally, one can try to make it impossible for the other person to act differently from what one thinks best by laying hands on him, locking the door, hiding the car keys, and so on. Here words are no longer the tool, and final decisions (however stacked by threats or bribes or misrepresentations) are no longer left to the intended beneficiary.

A first point is that none of these tactics is necessarily free of arrogance. Even in giving warning, one assumes oneself to know something the other party does not. That could be justified, of course, but it could also betray considerable arrogance about oneself. Neither is any of these measures necessarily arrogant, however. One more step and that photographer will be hit by that truck, so of course you lay hands on him, and there is no arrogance in the belief that you should do so. You may be wrong to think this is a better outcome for him, or that you knew something he did not. Such thoughts are not unjustified, however, and so you are not arrogant to enact them. Under different circumstances such beliefs might be arrogant, of course: here the point is only that even the most coercive measures can be free of this fault.

So humility does not set one resolutely against any of these measures as such, any more than it ensures that one will have no problem with some of them (the verbal ones, perhaps, where you are "only" talking). There are reasons to think that a humble person will favor the less coercive measures, though. That is, there are reasons to think that when several options are open a humble person will be more inclined to warn or to argue, for example, than to misinform or to threaten or to use force.

First: a measure is more coercive the less room it leaves for the possibility that you are wrong about how this person should act or about your being entitled to ensure that he does. The more coercive measures have an assurance about them, a confidence that might or might not match the mental state of the person who takes them. The assurance in a measure can be justified, of course, but it can also be misplaced in the way typical of arrogance. The truth can be that you have no business acting this confidently but ought to take a course that leaves more room for your being wrong.

The greater the gap between the assurance in your measure and your grounds for thinking it legitimate, the more extensively you will have overstepped yourself, and the more arrogant your behavior will be. Accordingly, a more coercive measure will be more arrogant than a less coercive one taken on the same basis, even if the lesser one also turns out to be arrogant. For, the more coercive measure will overstep to a greater degree. Recall, though, that a humble person is more repelled by greater arrogance than by lesser and wants, if possible, to avoid arrogance altogether. So, as a rule, he will be more leery of the more coercive measures when he feels he must act paternalistically and more inclined toward the less coercive ones.

A different argument to that same conclusion would run as follows. It may happen fairly often that we are entitled to think we have information someone else lacks, or a better understanding of how that information bears on the right decision. In contrast, we would only rarely be justified in thinking ourselves so much better informed that we should ensure that a certain course is followed. The more coercive the measure, the closer it comes to doing exactly that. To put it briefly, we are much more often justified in thinking ourselves able to contribute to someone's behavior than we are in thinking ourselves entitled to control it. Humility involves understanding the limits of one's expertise and one's proper role. So, a humble person would be more inclined to "contributory" paternalism than to its more controlling forms. He would be more inclined, that is, to talk and to argue than to use force, lies, or threats.

Notice too that some efforts to act paternalistically are not over in an instant, on the model of steering an unwary pedestrian out of the path of a truck. Instead, they take time. They may begin with talk, for example, but the talk may go on, becoming more heated, perhaps ending in different strategies such as threats, bribes, or force. The paternalist's persistence in these sequences can be arrogant, in the same way as the imagined political theorist's persistence is in managing the departmental picnic despite mounting evidence that he is not really the person to do this.

Mounting evidence that you are not the person to determine what course is in someone's best interest could take many forms. It could emerge that her own favored alternative has quite a lot to be said for it, after all, or that you know much less about the situation than you thought, or that your help is simply unwelcome. To persevere in insisting that she see things your way and that she act accordingly is to overreach yourself, quite possibly out of the kind of general self-elevation that constitutes arrogance. We should expect a humble person to know fairly well when to stop, as well as to have a light hand at the outset.

5

It is worth noting in passing that the place humility makes for paternalism is not the same as would be made by distinguishing between "hard" and "soft" paternalism and swearing off

the hard stuff. The hard/soft distinction, credited to Joel Feinberg, is between (hard) intervention, undertaken "to protect
fully competent adults, against their will, from the harmful
consequences even of their fully voluntary undertakings" and
(soft) intervention, undertaken when the person's "apparent
choice stems from ignorance, coercion, derangement, drugs, or
other voluntariness-vitiating factors," so that "there are grounds
for suspecting that it does not come from his own will, and
might be as alien to him as the choices of someone else."[8]

Feinberg himself regards hard paternalism as arrogant,
among other things, and suggests that soft paternalism will be
congenial to those who want to evade the objectionability of
hard paternalism without giving up "apparently reasonable"
paternalism.[9] Whatever one thinks of that proposal, it would
be wrong to think that paternalism will be free of arrogance so
long as it is soft. One obvious concern about an act of soft
paternalism would be the agent's basis for considering someone else to be in a defective state, as compared to herself. Why
does she believe this person to be ignorant of important facts
that she herself knows, for example? Plainly, there could be
arrogance in her thinking this. That arrogance would be present even though the soft paternalist was trying only to prevent someone's making a choice he would not make if he were
in a different state of mind.

There may also be arrogance in imposing one's own cautious style, by insisting that further information be gathered
before a decision is made. This extends, I think, to the case in
which the other party would decide differently if he had the
information but also does not in general entirely regret making
ill-informed decisions. He prefers leaping to plodding, that is,
even though he agrees that when he plods he reaches different
decisions and sometimes ones with which he is happier later.
His choice this time stems from ignorance, just as you think,
but also from his personality. There is nothing that entitles
you to insist that he act in accordance with your personality

instead. To do so would be arrogant, and therefore repellent to a person of humility.

Consider next a distinction that applies regardless of whether it is soft or hard paternalism under consideration: it makes a difference whether the person you mean to help is a friend or a stranger. For example, suppose someone has drunk a little too much and is beginning to make a fool of herself. It would be a lot better for her if she would stop, but she shows no sign of doing so: she will not feel humiliated until much later. You could try to settle her down in some way and save her that embarrassment, as an act of soft paternalism. Or, you could leave her alone.

It seems to make a considerable difference here whether this woman is a stranger or a friend of yours. If she is a stranger, an effort to stop her from embarrassing herself would be at most an act of kindness, and at worst none of your business. If she is a friend, however, she might well be entitled to expect you to help her at times like these. Were you to back off, she might be entitled to ask later why you had not stepped in, whereas a stranger would not be entitled to any such explanation. Where soft paternalism is concerned, it seems, a friend's welfare is more your business than a stranger's.

The same goes for hard paternalism. Consider unhealthy practices, undertaken not through lack of information or psychological impairment or coercion but (apparently) just as a matter of taste and personality. For example, high cholesterol diets are now widely taken to pose various risks to one's life. It is pretty clearly unhealthy to eat this way, but a great many of us do it anyway, despite being more or less aware of this. To what extent do you have a duty to keep after such people, doing your argumentative best to persuade them to drop those french fries, replace that butter with margarine and that ice cream with sherbert, and so on?

Again, it seems to matter whether it is a friend or a stranger you are trying to help. Zeal in such matters is intrusive: who are you to bend my ear and demand to know how I can act so stupidly? The question has a place, and "I am your friend" can be a suitable answer.

In short, there are contexts in which paternalism toward friends differs from paternalism toward strangers, regardless of whether the paternalism is soft or hard. A measure that would be at best supererogatory and at worst intrusive if taken toward a stranger can be at least acceptable and perhaps even obligatory if taken toward a friend.

Since we care about our friends more extensively and more intensely than we care about strangers, we are also more inclined to look after them. But surely the fact that we care more is not the reason that we have a greater responsibility here. Caring passionately about you cannot put you in my charge, so to speak, if there is anything at all to the idea of autonomy as a thing of value. And it is possible for even a friend to go too far in her paternalism—the fact that she cares deeply about someone is not carte blanche to guide that friend's life, even when the feelings are mutual.

What determines when paternalism toward friends has gone too far, despite its being motivated by affectionate concern? What is it that makes paternalism toward friends different from paternalism toward strangers? Why is it that although some friends would be entitled to be upset with you for not stopping them from continuing to embarrass themselves, others might be just as offended by your efforts as if they were strangers? The answers connect nicely with the theme of humility and arrogance.

The first point is that friendships are relationships that the particular friends make, with their own distinctive rules and expectations. What is expected, what is permitted, what goes too far depends on the parties involved and on certain events in the history of the friendship. It begins roughly as follows: because friends care about each other's well-being, their concern eventually finds expression in action. A friend offers sympathy when things are not going well or responds to a request for help or offers help unasked.

It is possible for the second friend to reject this expression of concern, but let us suppose she accepts it. That acceptance invites more of the same, both on this occasion and on future occasions of a similar kind. Moreover, in expressing his concern, the first friend invites the second to reciprocate, should their positions ever be reversed.

Accordingly, when future occasions do arise the new expression of concern has the status of having been invited. That makes it different from the same act performed by a stranger. The stranger has not been invited to care about one this deeply or to express his concern in this way. He might be welcome to do so, perhaps as the start of another friendship, but he also might not be. He has not been entitled to act in this way by one's invitation to do so. Insofar as (unlike the friend) he has no justification for thinking himself so entitled, his behavior (unlike the friend's) is arrogant.

This extends to expressions of concern that are paternalistic. These too can be morally inoffensive when enacted by friends who have been invited to treat one in this way, and offensively arrogant when enacted by strangers who have not. What about friends who have not been invited to go quite this far?

Sometimes, that is the oversolicitous friendly paternalism mentioned earlier. Other times, though, it represents a deepening of the relationship: we were friends, sort of, but then you did much more to help me than I had any reason to expect, and we have been much closer since . . . The difference seems to be in whether the efforts to help were, if not quite *invited* (in the loose way described), at least something it was reasonable to believe might be welcome. The friend who is not being pushy may be rewarded for his sense of how things might go by having the relationship deepen. The friend who is being pushy may get the opposite reaction, after having plowed ahead without benefit of signs.

The trickiness of gauging this recommends that any steps that might either deepen or disrupt a relationship (because uninvited) be tentative rather than bold. One kind of friendly paternalism that goes too far does so by going too fast, in a sense. A more distressing kind involves a friend who has been told a thousand times not to do this sort of thing and who persists in doing it anyway: *against* the signs, rather than just without benefit of them. There is an obliviousness in this that we could plausibly connect to arrogance. This second friend is making wholly unreasonable assumptions that the shape of your relationship is up to him or that really you must agree that his way is best or that only his wishes matter. That is arrogant in itself and may betray a deeper arrogance in his conception of his intelligence, attractiveness, or general place in the universe.

In sum, friendly paternalism that goes too far is like the paternalism of a stranger in its being uninvited. It differs from paternalism that serves to deepen the relationship by being not only uninvited but also unwelcome. Friendly paternalism that goes too far is at its most objectionable when it is so clearly unwelcome that forcing it on someone represents arrogance. We can expect, then, that humility would work against both intrusive paternalism toward strangers and the most objectionable paternalism toward friends.

It is also possible for two friends to be clear that paternalistic attention is not only welcome but expected, that it is part of this relationship that they look after each other in this way. In that case, to fail to do so is to disappoint an expectation. And, while it is not always wrong to disappoint expectations, it is wrong to do this when one has nurtured the expectation (think of breaking a promise). That provides a sense in which it can be wrong not to look after a friend in a way in which it would be improper to look after a stranger: namely, because you have disappointed an expectation you nurtured in the one case and stepped in uninvited in the other.

One nurtures such expectations by continuing in a relationship in which one knows them to exist, without clarifying matters. Not every pair of friends is alike in such expectations, of course, any more than every pair is alike in the specific permissions extended by their actions and reactions. So, the obligations to act paternalistically toward one's friend are not identical from friendship to friendship, just as the range of merely permissible paternalism is not the same.

The broader connection between all this and humility runs as follows. First, the fact that you have been invited to act in a certain way does a great deal to free your doing so from arrogance. Admittedly, there are invitations one ought not to accept, in that accepting them endorses a picture of oneself as something one clearly is not. For example, even though we have invited you to solve all of our university's problems, it might still be arrogant for you to think that you could do so. The hypothesis that you could solve them all could remain ridiculous, that is, in the same way as the hypothesis that Nelson was divine remained ridiculous despite public adulation of him. Invitations, like adulation, no doubt encourage one to believe certain things of oneself, but they do not necessarily make them reasonable to believe. So, it can be arrogant to do something even though one has been invited to do it: accepting some invitations is itself an act of arrogance.

At least, this is true if you accept the invitations without reservations, in full confidence that you can do the clearly impossible. To accept without such illusions is an entirely different story: no arrogance here on your part, since no unreasonable confidence in yourself. The same is true when the invited task is one it would not be unreasonable to think you could accomplish.

I think that most of the invitations to paternalism in a normal friendship can be accepted without arrogance, in that they ask only for help of manageable kinds. A friend who expected more would not be a friend for long, surely, and perhaps seeks a different relationship than friendship. Where the tasks you are invited to undertake are reasonable ones, I want to suggest, the fact that you are responding to an invitation transforms the undertaking. It means you are not arrogating this role to yourself out of some condescending sense of noblesse oblige but merely acting as requested.

Compare here a person who comes to your party without having been invited, and a person who comes because you invited her. The gate crasher may believe that invitations are for peons, not for those who are above petty rules and restrictions. Or, perhaps his thought is only that it would please him to go and this is all that matters; or, that any failure to invite him can only be an oversight, and certainly not in the best interests of the other guests. The person who comes because she has been invited is free of these various forms of arrogance.

The same goes for looking after someone because he has invited you to do so. To look after someone "because he is my friend" is, in part, to do so because he has invited me to do this. It is also, in part, to do so because I have led him to expect that I will. That too frees my behavior from the arrogance it could have if it enacted an assumption that everyone wants my attention and tender concern. The signs are pretty plain that many would prefer I left them alone.

Accordingly, the distinction between acting paternalistically toward friends and acting paternalistically toward strangers is one a person of humility would find natural. It cuts in a way that suits his being repelled by arrogance. Not, of course, that humility would interfere with helping strangers when it would *not* be arrogant to do so. No special invitation is needed to be helpful in some dramatic ways; or, to put it differently, we should assume a standing invitation to keep each other from eating contaminated food, stepping off piers, and the like. There is no arrogance in doing so, and hence no special difficulty in it for a person of humility.

6

Humility stands in the way of certain acts of paternalism, even if they are motivated by the purest good will toward the person in question. It stands in the way of perfectionism for the same reason: namely, that these actions are arrogant. Humility also inclines one toward less coercive measures, when the only question is what form of paternalism is to be employed. It inclines one to treat friends differently from strangers, to treat some friends differently from others, and to be cautious in taking steps that might either deepen or disrupt a relationship: all because there is arrogance in acting otherwise.

Those are considerable benefits, I think, but the aversion to arrogance also has costs. It is conceivable that an arrogant action could be the best thing to do on balance. A humble person would not be quick off the mark at such times and might even be unable to bring himself to do this thing at all, so that some less than optimal course was followed instead.

Still, to have an aversion to something is only to be disposed against it, not wholly incapable of doing it. Whatever made an arrogant course "the best thing to do on balance" would be there for the humble person to attend to, just as it is for those who lack humility. There is no reason to assume it could not overcome his disposition against the course. What humility does is to make it difficult to act arrogantly. Where paternalism is concerned, that is not a bad posture, all things considered.

This chapter casts the humble person as the agent of paternalism. A different set of questions arises if we cast him instead as the subject of paternalistic attentions. Does humility mean a greater willingness to accept such attentions, perhaps out of an awareness that one is not necessarily right about which course must be in one's own best interest? The next chapter takes this matter up, in the context of major decisions about one's life.

6

"IT'S MY LIFE!"

The patient has a serious illness but prefers to leave it untreated. Others press her to accept treatment. Does she have the right to reject their urgings?

One argument that she does have this right is compressed in an exclamation she might make: "It's my life!" The point of the exclamation is that this makes the choice hers as well. Others might choose differently if they were in her position, but (her argument goes) that is irrelevant. This time it is she who should decide, because this time it is her life about which the decision is to be made.

This argument can be very compelling. Who are we to insist that someone must spend her last days in the cancer center, enduring the latest technology, rather than at home with her family? A dictum of John Stuart Mill's comes to mind: "Neither one person, nor any number of persons, is warranted in saying to another human being of ripe years that he shall not do with his own life for his own benefit what he chooses to do with it."[1] And yet, it is also the patient's life when he is not terminally ill and could easily be kept from dying. Here is one such case, deeply disturbing to the philosopher who offers it.

141

> A thirty-eight-year-old man with mild upper respi-
> ratory infection suddenly developed severe head-
> ache, stiff neck, and high fever. . . . The diagnosis
> was pneumococcal meningitis, a bacterial menin-
> gitis almost always fatal if not treated. If treatment
> is delayed, permanent neurological damage is likely.
> A physician told the patient that urgent treatment
> was needed to save his life and forestall brain dam-
> age. The patient refused to consent to treatment,
> saying that he wanted to be allowed to die.[2]

Should his wishes be honored? After all, it is his life that is in
question, every bit as fully as it was the cancer victim's life,
when she wanted to end her days at home rather than in the
hospital. If that is her decision because, after all, it is her life,
should this be his decision because, after all, it is his?

The cases can be multiplied. There are diabetics who
simply refuse to look after themselves properly, even though
this threatens and certainly shortens their lives. There are
heart patients who refuse to exercise, and elderly people who
are so repelled by the prospect of failing powers and uncomfortable days that they prefer to end their lives rather than
continue them. In each case, it is this person's life that the
decision is about. Does that mean the decision should be
theirs to make? Or does "It's *my* life!" have limits, which these
people exceed in some way?

One appealing position is that this depends entirely on
whether the patient is rational. If not, he or she does not have
the usual authority; if so, we are entitled only to delay the
patient's decision in hopes of affecting it through information,
argument, and perhaps bribery or threats. Should those efforts
fail to persuade a competent person to our view of the proper
decision, we must stand aside and allow this person to decide
as he or she wishes, on this view: even in the cases described.

I cannot consider here whether this position treats incompetent people as it should.[3] I will restrict myself instead to persons whose competence is not in doubt, that is: to the idea that competent people are to have the final authority to make the decisions exemplified because their lives are the subjects of those decisions. I am interested particularly in a person's asserting this authority, and whether that can ever be a failure of humility. Suppose the advice of professionals is very much to the contrary; or suppose friends and family urge you not to make the choice you prefer; or suppose your choice will bear greatly on their lives as well as shape your own. Would it ever be a failure of humility to insist on having it your way, on the sole ground that it is your life about which you are choosing?

I do not mean here insisting on your choice on the ground that is the wiser one—for example, that whatever these doctors say, you know better which treatment will work best. Clearly, that stance can be an arrogant one, when it is not a terrified denial of the facts. I mean instead insisting that regardless of whether it is the wisest choice, it is to be your choice because it is your life. I mean demanding that you have things your way because you are the one who will be going down that way. Is there ever a lack of humility in that sort of insistence or demand, or is this never any more than claiming your due?

The answer largely depends, I think, on what a person's life is, and what our relationship is to our lives. It also depends on what follows from the fact that lives can be so intertwined that it is impossible greatly to affect one life without greatly affecting another. I will begin by describing what sort of thing a life is and then explore several conceptions of what it is for a particular life to be yours. This provides a basis for understanding the interest we have in leading our lives, and thus for considering when it is unhumble to assert that interest as if it were decisive, and when it is not.

1

One part of a person's life consists in what that person does. In each life there is public behavior and there are mental acts: there is walking to the library, but also daydreaming as you do so; there is sitting at the table, but also remembering that you are late; there is tripping over the chair, but also thinking black thoughts about it.

Actions are not independent of each other but interrelated, of course. We perform some of them because we performed others earlier (in atonement, in gratitude, in order to keep a promise). Others are parts of projects, as walking to the library might be part of an exercise program. Even the walking itself is a series of actions, though to call it a project would be misleading. The general point is that what I am doing at any given moment can depend in part on what I mean to do later, as well as on what I have done earlier.

It also depends on a good deal else. Because of local customs, my going to the library now might indicate friendly feelings toward someone who is always there at this same time. (This is not a function of my intentions; going in order to indicate interest would be something else again.) Depending on the causal prospects of my behavior, I might also be risking damage to my reputation by going at this time, improving my chances for completing some work I have under way, and so on. Depending on how things actually turn out, I might be starting a friendship with the librarian or a new phase of my career.

In sum, it would be very wrong to picture the part of our lives that consists in what we do as a string of independent events. Instead, there are interconnections of many kinds, which hold because actions have backgrounds, motivation, causal prospects, and actual outcomes and occur in cultural contexts. In part, to live is to do. Exactly what we are doing has many determinants, however, only some of which are further actions of our own.

The same is true of the experiences a person has. Sometimes, their dependence is straightforwardly causal: you smell cut grass because you are mowing the lawn; you are sore because you used muscles that you do not normally use. Sometimes, matters are more complicated: which experiences you have depends partly on what you are expecting, where your attention is focused. If you have set out to find a particular restaurant, you look for what bears on finding it. That may mean you miss the glorious sunset—though not all pursuit of a plan is equally single-minded and absorbing. Then, too, you may have a certain history with a person or a place, so that you no longer notice things that strike those for whom they arc frcsh, and (pcrhaps) you see instead some things a new person would overlook.

There are limits, of course. Some events demand your attention, distracting you from whatever you had under way: that truck ran over your foot; those people are stark naked. There are also differences in personal style, in how easily one is distracted in general and in which things are more absorbing. The point is that although your experiences (like your actions) are certainly part of your life, which experiences you have (like which actions you perform) will have various determinants, only some of which are within your control. A life is not a thing apart from the rest of the world, but something lived in it; how far you shape it yourself is a matter of degree.

Finally, what might be called the biological processes of your body are also part of your life, vital though uninteresting as long as they continue smoothly along. You digest your Mexican dinner, your eyes adjust to the light, you inhale and exhale, and so on. For the most part these are things your organs and systems do, without any direct help from you. They are not experiences you have, though they can give rise to experiences.

Their being part of one's life produces the following complication. At the end of a person's life, there may be a period during which the body works in these ways and the person has experiences but performs no actions. Or, there may be a period during which she neither acts nor has experiences but *only* has biological processes. Perhaps these periods befall only those in very deep comas. Perhaps, instead, they are a usual stage of dying. Perhaps there are such periods in fetal development, as well. The question is, should we consider these parts of the person's life, because the body is working then? Or, should we hold that they are not, either because no *person* exists at such times or because that kind of existence is not *life*?

The answer is far from obvious. It depends, for one thing, on what it is to be a person: whether a deeply comatose individual would count as a person and could therefore be the *same* person now living on in a drastically limited way. It also depends on whether a person can live on as something of a different kind, so that even if the deeply comatose are no longer persons they might still be the same individuals in a different, nonpersonal stage of their lives. We would also need a theory of identity, if we are to say whether the cutting of some thread of psychological continuity means we no longer have the same individual as we had before.

Without a full-scale theory of personhood and self-identity, then, there are some things we will not be able to decide about the argument encapsulated in "It's my life!" We will not be able to say whether it extends to "It is I who will be living on in a deep coma." Perhaps it *is* I, and my advanced directives about what is to happen should have the corresponding force (whatever that turns out to be). Perhaps it is *not* I, and such directives should only have whatever force derives from my special relationship to the new individual in the bed (at least as much force as my directives about my corpse or my faithful pets, presumably, but perhaps not as much as my directives about myself—particularly if the new individual should be considered a different person than I once was).

In the same way, without a theory of personhood and self-identity, we cannot say whether those who become permanently insane in various ways are continuing to live their lives, or have ceased to exist and have been replaced by someone or something else. Accordingly, we could not say whether their earlier wishes about how their lives should go have the same force when applied to the existence of the unfortunate creature in the asylum, or, if they had never discussed this explicitly, how urgently we should try to work out how they would prefer their lives to go if they had spoken.

Unfortunately, there is no obviously correct view to take about personhood and self-identity. The issues are sharply argued, and there are good arguments for competing positions. The wisest course seems to be to remain silent about the matters above, where the individual's personhood and identity are too uncertain for us to say whether something is part of a certain individual's life. Perhaps philosophy will advance so that this silence need not be permanent.

For now, we can still consider cases of the kind with which this chapter began, despite taking no position on the deeply comatose, the greatly deranged, and their ilk. For, in our cases, there is no doubt that we are dealing with a person and with the question how that person's life is to continue. For example, there is no question that a diabetic who chose to forego her insulin would still be a person, and a person who was living her life in a particular way, or that the elderly person who decides on suicide is a person who is deciding to bring his life to a close. Nor does every kind of brain damage cast doubt on personal identity, or on whether the individual is still a person at all.

Finally, consider the woman who wants to abandon her cancer therapy and die at home. For most of her decline, once again there can be no serious question that it is she who is declining, and thus that her wishes about the course of her life have whatever force such wishes have. One difficulty remains:

it could be that the last stages of dying involve an existence in which various organic systems function but the individual neither does anything nor experiences anything. Since we have not worked out whether this stage is part of one's life or is post-humous, should we not be at a loss about whether (even though *this* person wanted to be allowed to die) we should allow her decision to dictate the death of the individual in the bed?

Not really. The thought that there might be a period like this is purely hypothetical. It is not as if we can tell that someone is in such a period and must therefore take very seriously the question whose life we might be allowing to end. The plausible course is to act as if it were still she in the bed. Accordingly, the plausible course is to afford her wish to die whatever authority such wishes have, rather than to act as if the process of dying includes a change of identity before it is completed.

In sum, our situation is this. There are matters we cannot decide without a full-scale theory of personhood and self-identity. These include whether a period in which certain organic systems function but the individual neither does nor experiences anything would be part of a person's life. Such a theory is hard to come by. Fortunately, however, it seems possible to think about more standard cases without one.

I propose, then, to leave the matter unsettled and to think of someone's life as the sequence of that person's actions and experiences and at least those biological processes that occur after his or her first experience or action and before his or her last. As noted, the elements of the sequence are not independent but interrelated in several ways that help define the content of the life. On this definition lives are also informed by events and states of affairs that are not part of them: by wars, economic events, social mores, and so on. For those too bear on what one does and what experiences one has.

On this view, other people and their actions are not parts of one's life, despite their impact on what sort of life it is, since they are not among one's actions or experiences or the workings of one's body. This may be startling. It may seem very strange to say that even someone you love, someone with whom you spend a great deal of your time and around whom you build a great deal of your life, is not actually any part of it. There are good reasons to say exactly this, however.

Suppose instead that other people were, literally, parts of your life. Presumably this would not be a matter of their being contained entirely within it, like the proverbial fly in amber. Instead, they would be parts of your life only insofar as they affected it or were affected by it. In this way they could be parts of many lives, and in the larger part of their existence not part of yours at all. Thus, most of what your spouse and son did all day would not be part of your life, since the causal connections would be missing, but your spouse's earning the money you spend would be, as would your son's following your advice.

This might seem plausible enough. Unfortunately, though, such connections hold at impossibly awkward times. Suppose it were not your spouse who earned most of the money you spend but your grandfather, a man who died before you were conceived. He and his career would have the same impact on your actions and experiences as your spouse and her career do now, and thus the same claim to be part of your life. But surely he and his deeds cannot be part of your life, since they had their existence long before your life began. Similarly, suppose that fifteen years after your death your son finally sees the point of your arguments and takes up the family business. How could his doing so be part of your life, which ended years earlier?

We could try to preserve the idea that other people and their behavior are parts of one's life. We could say (bravely) that actually a person's life begins much earlier than is commonly thought and goes on long after he is, as we say, dead and buried. Or, we could try something ad hoc: other people are parts of one's life only insofar as these connections hold while one is acting and experiencing, not before or after.

I think it is more appealing to think of a person's life as his or her own actions, experiences, and biological processes, with other people and larger events pictured as affecting it from the outside. There is nothing odd about saying your grandfather's getting rich had a great deal to do with what sort of life you lead, as there is about saying that he and his getting rich are parts of your life. Nor is it odd to say that your son's taking up the business after you died made your life less futile, unlike saying that his doing this is part of your life despite your being dead when it occurs. Connections of these kinds have enormous impact on what a person's life is like; to say they have their impact "from the outside" does not overlook this or minimize its importance.

If that is what your life is, what is it for a particular life to be yours? The next section explores three answers to this peculiar-sounding question.

2

One view about the matter is that our lives are our property, belonging to us in the same way as anything else that we own. John Locke offered something along these lines: "Every man has a property in his own person; this nobody has any right to but himself.[4] James Rachels refers to a similar position, in writing about euthanasia: "A person's life is, quite literally, all he has; and so the value of his life, to him, is beyond calculation."[5]

Suppose our lives were our property, owned by us in the same way as you own your shirt. On at least some views of ownership, this would make "It's *my* life!" a powerful claim indeed. For, on those views, it is part of ownership that one has the right to keep what one owns in the condition one prefers it and to destroy it when it no longer pleases one. An owner need not have particularly good reasons: if she has simply grown tired of her old shirt, that is justification enough for her tearing it to shreds.[6] If her life were hers in the same way, she would have this same authority over it.

Of course, she could not replace her life as she could her shirt, so it would trouble us if she took its condition and destruction equally lightly. Still, deciding to destroy her life rather than to alter it would be well within her rights, on this view, since the right to destroy what we own is part of owning it.

It might be objected that although the right to destroy your property is part of owning relatively trivial items such as shirts, it is not part of owning something more substantial. For example, you are not free to destroy your house, because this could ruin the value of neighboring houses. Even so, it is still your house. Just so, destroying a life might ruin neighboring lives, it seems. Perhaps we own our lives in this more restricted way?

If so, we might still have considerable authority to end them. After all, it is not necessarily wrong to destroy your house without your neighbors' consent: you are perfectly free to do so, as long as you offer your neighbors fair compensation for their loss. So, on this model, you would be equally free to end your life without the consent of anyone else, as long as you offered fair compensation (whatever that would be). What is more, anyone whose demise would not diminish the lives of others would be free of even this limitation.

Actually, however, there seem to me to be insurmountable problems with both forms of the view that our lives are something we own. The trouble is that to own something is to be entitled not only to destroy it but also to sell it, or to give it away. This might appear to pose a serious moral problem. After all, if you were to sell someone your life the new owner would gain not only your labor but everything, including whatever right you now have to end this life if it no longer pleases. Any view that legitimizes such complete subjugation will strike some as morally unacceptable.

In truth, the view has faults of a deeper kind: the very idea of passing your life on to someone else is nonsense. To transfer ownership of something is to put someone else in the position you now have to it. It was yours; it becomes his in the same way. But it is impossible to put someone else in the relation to your life you now have in living it. Once you are not living it, your life is over. It does not go on as-lived-by-some-one-else, like a play starring a new actor.

The reason for this is that what makes a life yours is its being the one *you* live. A life is nothing but a particular sequence of actions, experiences, and biological processes. For it to be your life is just for you to be the one whose actions, experiences, and biological processes make it up. This means lives are not transferrable, and that means we ought not to think of them as something we own.

This conclusion will please those who never cared much for the implications of the ownership view in the first place. For example, some disapprove wholeheartedly of suicide and voluntary euthanasia, precisely because they think that our lives do not belong to us, but are only ours in trust. On their view, "a person's life is conceived as belonging, not to himself, but to God. That is why life is not like property; that is why a person may not dispose of his life on his own authority."[7]

Notice, in passing, that this is distinct from the view that our lives are God's gifts to us, which we would be ungrateful to destroy. If our lives were gifts, they would be ours; on the view quoted, they remain God's. Our position is that of a care-taker of God's property, obliged to treat it as instructed while it is in our trust and to keep it until it is called for.

I believe that these ways of thinking come to grief over the same point as the ownership view: the fact that you are the only one who can have the relationship you have to your life. In contrast, anything placed in one person's care could have been entrusted to another. But no one else could have had your life; whatever anyone else had would have been a different life, resembling yours, perhaps, but still distinct.

Moreover, anything put in one person's care could be entrusted to several: "caretaker" is a job that can be held jointly. The same holds for anything given as a gift: it could have been given to several people to share. Thus, if our relation to our lives were one of these, then several people could have lived your life at once, instead of your having to go it alone. That might sound companionable, but actually it is confused. At most, your life could have lacked some of what it has (your marrying a particular person) and someone else's life could have had something like it (their marrying that person). This is not a way in which two people live somehow jointly but only one in which their separate lives are different from what they were.

In sum, the argument has been that it is inconceivable for more than one person to live your life, or for someone else to have had the whole thing to herself. Those things would be conceivable if living a life consisted in holding someone else's property in trust or in having it as a gift. So, these are not the right ways to think about what it is for a life to be yours, just as it is not appropriate to think of this as your *owning* the life in question.

3

> "In life," he said, "there are essentially no major or minor characters. . . . Everyone is necessarily the hero of his own life story. *Hamlet* could be told from Polonius' point of view and called *The Tragedy of Polonius, Lord Chamberlin of Denmark.*"[8]

When Tom Stoppard turned this particular trick, he rewrote *Hamlet* not from the point of view of Polonius but from that of Rosencrantz and Guildenstern. His play, *Rosencrantz and Guildenstern Are Dead*, contains episodes not recounted in

Hamlet, but mostly it consists in what we might call the *same* events as they impinge on the lives of these two men. We see Hamlet's behavior through their eyes, have their perspective on their delivery of their fatal message, and so on. It all rings very true.

It also seems congenial to the idea that each person's life is the series of his or her own actions and experiences. So, shall we think of living as being the central figure of a play, rather than as owning some object or having it in one's care? The idea is not without appeal. A play, like a life, is a series of events rather than an object. Perhaps that will take us past the objection that lives are not transferrable, as objects are. For, like a life, a play without its central character would not be the same play: think of *Hamlet* without Hamlet, or *Rosencrantz and Guildenstern Are Dead* without Rosencrantz. Moreover, lives also resemble plays in that each takes much of its shape from the continuing relationships between the lead character and the other characters. Your life without those dearest to you would be a very different life, just as *Hamlet* would be a very different play without Gertrude.

Plays, however, have many characters—hence the distinction between major and minor ones—while lives, I have argued, have only one. Worse, we can only take the comparison to a play literally if we accept absolute determinism. After all, no character in a play does anything on his own, really, not even the hero. To put it differently, some of what a character does is the playwright's doing, some is the director's, and some is the actor's, working under these influences and those of the audience and the other actors. Any sense in which the character "comes alive" is purely metaphorical, a way people speak when the playing is especially vivid and coherent or when some of these influences are so compelling that various bits of behavior seem absolutely right for this character. The literal truth is that the characters are entirely the creatures of those who write and play them, and they do nothing themselves.

Well, perhaps life *is* like this, and it's just that I've forgotten all my lines? That would explain why others often seem so much less awkward, so much more aware of what is called for. . . . But it would also make me an actor, rather than a character. That would restore the power to originate action, but it would also mean that I was not essential: unlike a main character, an actor can be replaced without making it a different play. As argued earlier, we *are* essential to our lives; so, it will not do to think of us as actors either.

Still, even if all this means we do not want to take literally the remark quoted from John Barth's novel, perhaps it is an illuminating metaphor? Perhaps living a life is *like* being a lead character, in important ways? The lead character, I take it, is the figure around whom most of the main action in the play revolves. He or she initiates most of what advances the plot, that is, with the other characters serving to set the stage, to react, and to engage in various subplots.

We might want to resist saying that living is much like this, on the ground that there is no "main action" to our lives, nothing resembling a *plot* to them. Instead, our lives seem to happen in bits and stretches, with only some parts of them initiating anyone's plan. But we do speak comfortably of major events in a person's life: leaving home, marrying, taking up a certain line of work, retiring, and so on. These are events with extensive reverberations within the life, opening some possibilities, foreclosing others, affecting choices among what remains possible. We could think of those events and their train as the "main action," without having to imagine any master plot unifying the whole. Then the idea would be that to live a life is to be responsible for more of this main action than anyone else is. Is this a sense in which we *are* each necessarily the main character in our lives?

It is hard to be sure, since the criteria for main action are vague. Perhaps, instead, a person could live a life largely shaped by a few others. We think this is true of small children, for example, and of adults who continue to be dominated by their parents, and perhaps of a certain kind of person who moves directly from a parent's control to a spouse's. So it seems entirely possible that David has it right at the start of *David Copperfield*: "Whether I shall turn out to be the hero of my own life, or whether that status shall be held by anybody else, these pages must show."[9]

4

What is certain about lives turns out to be very simple. A life is nothing more than a series of actions, experiences, and biological processes, given unity by being the actions, experiences, and biological processes of a particular person. One's relation to one's life is not that of owner or caretaker or lead character, but simply that of the person whose actions (etc.) make it up. In this sense, we are necessarily the central figures in our own lives, everything in them involving us.

In the further sense of being responsible for the events that give our lives their shape, we are not all equally central. We differ, that is, in how much of the main action is our doing, and how much of it is imposed from the outside. At one extreme lie Rosencrantz and Guildenstern, whose lives are very unsettling in the extent to which the men do not lead them. Watching their story is like watching two animated pieces of driftwood being moved along by currents and puffs of wind. They do originate some pointless diversions and plenty of gallows humor, but mostly their lives happen *to* them.

The spectacle can be distressing. We do not want to believe that secretly our own lives are just like theirs. We want the opportunity to shape our lives. We may not want actually to *do* all of the shaping, to make all the hard decisions and to have nothing "outside" to blame when things go wrong. And some of us may prefer to shape our lives indirectly, by manipulating others into making the decisions we want made. Others may believe it is really not their role to make certain of the decisions: whom to marry or whether to have a child, for example. Still, in whatever respects and after whatever fashion we do want to shape our lives, we all deeply prefer to have the power to do so.

Perhaps the efficient thwarting of this deep preference is part of what makes a thoroughly racist society so repugnant. Think of modern South Africa; or, on some accounts, of the America of a dozen years past (if not also of the current day). In these places, the thing about some individuals is: "They are black, and no other feature of personality or allegiance or ambition will so thoroughly influence how they will be perceived and treated by others, and the range and character of the lives that will be open to them."[10]

Of course, we cannot shape our lives exactly as we like. Each of us is endowed with only certain talents. We each live in an environment that nurtures some forms of growth and discourages others. One person's plans may simply be incompatible with those of others. These various facts of life do not mean that the limitations racism imposes are something its victims should just accept as their variety of the human lot, however. Instead these limitations make the victims' plight more claustrophobic, as the inevitably narrowed range of possibilities narrows still further.

The same deep preference for shaping one's own life is in play in the medical cases with which we began. The patient wants to choose the course to be followed because the choice shapes her life. Staying in the hospital fighting her cancer means living very differently from how she would if she were to go home, both in what she does and in what experiences she is likely to have. Similarly, to follow a diabetic's regimen is to live in a special way; and so on for the other examples. To make someone do these things is to shape that person's life.

So what? Suppose we grant that such choices do shape lives, and that we all have a deep preference for shaping our own lives ourselves. Others may have interests that can be served only if this preference is overridden: those who love us and those who depend on us, for example, as well as those who have an interest in the medically best course being followed. Can reasons be given why our interest in shaping our lives ought to prevail over these? If so, insisting on making such decisions is perfectly compatible with a humble person's reluctance to claim more than his due; if not, perhaps it is, after all, an act of arrogance.

We can start by considering more closely what our interest is in shaping our own lives. A natural first answer is that if we shape them we will have happier lives, since we know better than others what would be happiest for us, and thus our interest in making the big decisions is our interest in living as happily as we can. This is entirely adequate, for a number of cases. Often, that is, the conflicting interests of others are not remotely comparable. The answer also has well-known limitations, however, which are easy to illustrate in this context.

Suppose that the life you would have if you were to follow a certain course is very different from the one you have had so far, and that you will also experience some changes in your personality. Why would you be a better judge of how happy that life would be for the (relatively) new you than medical professionals, who have seen many such cases? We are not each *entirely* unlike all others, after all. Perhaps you are like a very young person thinking about what it must be like to be very old, and feeling sure you would not enjoy it. Perhaps, that is, you are too distant from this life to appreciate what it has to offer, or to understand that its lacking what you now relish is not like your suddenly being robbed of those things in the next five minutes.

The greater the chance of this, the weaker your credentials to decide whether you should live the life in question, if those credentials really did consist in your being the best judge of what would be happiest for you. You might have very

little claim of this kind, if the question were whether to un-
dergo brain surgery, whether to live on to develop a full case
of Alzheimer's disease, and so on. For, there are those who
know better than you do how content such people are, and
they might well be better judges of how happy you would be
in this state. That would make them the proper parties to decide which course your life followed, if the idea were to ensure that it followed the happiest course.

But, isn't this horrifying? Surely the fact that it is you
who will live this reduced existence remains a powerful reason to let you be the one who decides whether it is to be
lived? Surely it matters that you do not wish *your* future to
take a certain form even if (largely because you would not
then "know any better') you would be happy when the time
came? If these things do matter, we need a different explanation of why they do. Why else could it be that the patient
herself should choose what shape her life is to have? I think
the answer has four parts and describes a very strong interest
indeed in making such choices.

First, shaping our own lives is simply something we
deeply prefer to do, whenever we want to do it at all. To remind ourselves of this we need only ponder the Rosencrantzes
and Guildensterns of the world, who live so thoroughly at the
mercy of forces beyond their control. That we deeply prefer to
shape our own lives is itself a reason why we should do so,
distinct from the good consequences this might or might not
have.

Second, we each have only one life to lead, and we live
it, so to speak, in a straight line rather than a circle. Each part
of a life happens only once; if we are prevented from living it
as we would prefer, the chance to do so is lost forever. We do
sometimes get later chances to live similar stretches as we
would prefer to have lived earlier ones. That is clearly not the
same as a second chance to live precisely this period over
again, though, with precisely these people under precisely

these circumstances, and precisely as we are ourselves at present. Hence, there is a sense in which shaping someone's life against her will deprives that person of something irrecoverable, not just something she wants badly but can have later. The deprivation is not temporary—it is permanent.

Third, to understand ourselves we need evidence, and a great deal of this evidence is in our actions. Sometimes, to understand our actions we must see them unfold, see what it really was to choose to marry this person or to decline that operation. By understanding your actions you grasp something about yourself: you see that you are someone who would choose to do *this* under these circumstances. To block your choice denies you that evidence and thus interferes with your understanding yourself.

Finally, it is only insofar as we are allowed to make our own record in the world and to understand both that record and ourselves that we have a fair basis for judging ourselves. Self-esteem on such a basis is legitimate, and so is discontent with ourselves. When those attitudes are based instead in ignorance, they are not legitimate, even if the ignorance is due to our having been protected from making bad choices. We have a powerful interest in understanding ourselves, and in having our estimation of ourselves be accurate: in not living as a fool, that is, whether an arrogant fool or one who sadly underestimates himself.

Add this to our various other interests in being happy, in satisfying a deep preference, and in not losing irrecoverably a thing we deeply want, and the sum is an imposing set of interests we have in deciding *for ourselves* the courses our lives take. Any argument that it is unhumble to assert these interests, that we take ourselves too seriously in doing so, will have to cite something even more powerful that we should be able to see to take precedence over our concerns. In particular, an argument that a patient's decision should be overruled for his own good will be especially difficult to make out. It is not at all clear why one's interest in being alive, or in living longer rather than less long, would be stronger than this set of interests in living as one chooses. So, "It's my life!" turns out to be a very forceful reply to paternalistic compulsion in these matters—not because we own our lives, but because we have very strong interests in shaping them.

Consider next, however, the fact that two lives can be so intertwined that one life cannot be shaped without also shaping another. Can there be a failure of humility here, in insisting that the mutual shaping be done to my liking? Imagine, for example, a man whose wife is manic-depressive. He has not had the energy or the concentration to do as well in his profession as he would have liked; it has been virtually impossible for them to keep friends; and he has had to look after their children in ways he never envisioned. Lately his wife has been taking the lithium her current doctor prescribed, and things have been much easier for everyone. Now, though, she has stopped taking her pills and refuses adamantly to start again. She says they make her life excruciatingly flat and boring, and, as she says, "It's my life we are talking about."

So it is, but (one wants to say) it is his life as well. On the one hand, if she lives as she wants to, he must either climb back into the roller-coaster or desert her and strike out on his own, neither of which he wants to do. On the other hand, for him to have the life he wants rules out her having the life she wants. The question is not whether to overrule her "for her own good." The question is, when someone's life must be shaped against that person's will, whose is it to be?

Humility does not require that it be yours, it seems to me, or even that it be your inclination to defer rather than to assert your own interests. That would follow if humility involved taking ones own interests necessarily to be less important, or thinking it improper to claim one's due. Such connections might hold if being humble were the same thing as thinking very poorly of oneself, or if it involved a lack of self-respect. Being humble is not those things, however, nor does it involve in some other way the conviction that your part must be to yield, however important an interest you might have to assert.

We are speaking here of sacrificing oneself. Although neither the husband nor the wife in the example is asked to die so the other may live, both are asked to lay down their lives in a different way. Such sacrifices are heroic. One wonders, though, whether there are not also other cases in which one party's sacrifice is clearly not so great as the other's would be. If so, it would be selfish to insist on having your way—a self-ishness the other party might accept, perhaps, but even so a self-elevation we should expect to run counter to humility.

Suppose, for example, that the question is whether to compel your independent, aged parent to enter a regimented nursing home so that you will not have to stop by a few times a week. To do so would shape very extensively all the life the parent has remaining, counter to his preferences. The alternative shapes only slightly what is likely to be only a limited portion of your life. It does so against your will, and you do have an interest in shaping your own life as you see fit. Since you plainly have so much less to lose here than he has, though, it seems there would be some unhumble self-centeredness in asserting that interest.

Typically, the contrast would be less plain, however, as in the case of the manic-depressive woman and her husband. Presumably, being on lithium shapes many aspects of her life; presumably, being married to a manic-depressive shapes many aspects of his. Each must assume that following the other's wishes will define not just a limited period but the rest of the years life has to offer. Neither would demonstrate a lack of humility by choosing to live as he or she preferred rather than according to the other's preference. In neither case could we make an accusation of self-absorption, or speak of arrogantly overestimating one's entitlements.

This is not to deny that there would be something of value in thinking through the alternatives, to clarify what a choice would cost the other person if it were taken. Very often, when lives are closely entwined there are ties of affection, and understanding what it would cost someone you love if you were to live your life as you prefer can provide a compelling reason to change your mind. Not, again, that you would necessarily be selfish and unhumble if you did not change your mind: it is just that the knowledge can move you, as part of what this person means to you. Or, you can realize that it fails to move you; then you have a clearer understanding of your relationship and an occasion to decide whether to try to deepen it.

Evidently, the variables involved in how extensively the choices would shape the lives affected can clearly favor the person who is ill and wants to live out his life as he chooses, as in the case of the aging parent. However, they can also favor the other party instead. Even in a matter so personal as whether to end one's life, someone who is loved by others may not be right to do so. Although it is undeniably her life she is ending, the reverberations of her doing so can be so shattering to the lives of others that it would have been better for her to endure. For her also to be arrogant or self-absorbed in doing so would require that her claims be clearly outweighed by the claims of the others. That is imaginable, though only in a special case.

The more general conclusion is that it can be unhumble to assert the claims that rest on its being your life, but only when this assertion forecloses claims that are clearly even more powerful. That foreclosure will occur only rarely, because it is itself so powerful, representing the general interest we each have in being as happy as possible; our deep preference for writing our own story (quite apart from whether we do this happily); the sense in which every stretch of our lives is irreplaceable to us; and our need to see our major choices unfold if we are to understand ourselves and to live according to a correct conception of who we are.

In particular, the claim to shape one's life as one wishes outweighs the sort of claims put forward typically in acts of paternalism or perfectionism. On the one hand, it is therefore not a failure of humility to hold out against such efforts for no more reason than "It's my life." On the other hand, it is possible to ignore the extent to which one's choice shapes not only one's own life but also the lives of others. Those others have the same claim in play. Then to insist on having one's way can be a failure of humility, under certain circumstances.

THE
SIMPLE
LIFE

W_{hen} I have met an immigrant tottering under a bundle which contained
his all—looking like an enormous wen which had
grown out of the nape of his neck—I have pitied
him, not because that was his all, but because he
had all *that* to carry. If I have got to drag my trap, I
will take care that it be a light one and do not nip
me in a vital part. But perchance it would be wisest
never to put one's paw into it.[1]

Is it plausible to expect that a humble person would live the
simple life Henry David Thoreau envisions in this passage,
with any possessions limited to a few essentials and a dwelling that is clean but spare? Thoreau thought so, as can be seen
in his easy equation of humility with poverty: "Humility like
darkness reveals the heavenly lights. The shadows of poverty
and meanness gather around us, 'and lo! creation widens to
our view.'"[2]

   The association has a natural feel: a humble person
should live in a "humble dwelling," it seems, not opulently
but simply. A man of "humble means" will be one who has

little, and must "live humbly." Were we to visit him, we would expect only "humble fare" and "humble accomoda-tions." All of this suggests that humility calls for one to live with only the minimal necessities: "near to the bone," as Tho-reau put it.[3]

In this chapter I consider what truth there is in this asso-ciation. I begin by describing a tradition according to which humility certainly does require a person to live simply—in-deed, to live a life that is not merely simple but intentionally harsh. That tradition has so influenced our thinking about hu-mility that its influence may be the chief explanation for the associations noted between "humble" and "poor." The tradi-tion should not be taken to be authoritative on the matter, however, and thus our question is not so easily answered.

In the rest of the chapter I consider four arguments that stand apart from the tradition. The arguments maintain that humility would at least incline a person to live simply. The first argument derives from the manifest presence of misery in the world. The second contends that anyone who realized how utterly insignificant he was in the vastness of the uni-verse would entirely lack personal ambition and for that rea-son would live simply. The third maintains that to live well is a way of boasting about oneself and follows Thomas Aquinas in urging that boasting is foreign to a humble person's nature. The fourth maintains that a humble person would wish not even to come to the notice of others and takes this reticence to call for a simple life.

1

Humility, I have argued, should be understood in terms of having oneself in proper perspective. If you are humble, you understand yourself sufficiently clearly that you are disin-clined to exaggerate your talents, accomplishments, and gen-eral place in the larger flow of events. There is an important tradition according to which understanding such things means realizing that you deserve credit for nothing that is good about you and deserve blame for everything that is bad about you. Aquinas put it this way: "We may consider two things in man, namely that which is God's, and that which is man's. Whatever pertains to defect is man's; but whatever pertains to man's welfare and perfections is God's."[4] The entry on humility in the *New Catholic Encyclopedia* agrees: "All a person's good—nature and grace, being and action—is a gift of God's creative and salvific love,"[5] while "only deficiencies belong to man."[6] It would follow that there is no cause for personal pride in whatever is good about you, but only for gratitude over the particular gifts you have been given. There is also, of course, plenty of cause to be ashamed of yourself, since we are all variously "deficient" in personal character and in what we do.

That is what all humble people would know when they understood themselves, on this view of what we are all like. Regardless of who I am, as Ignatius Loyola puts it, to understand myself would be "to look upon myself as a wound and ulcer whence have come forth so many sins and so many iniquities, and poison so utterly foul."[7] Now, this picture would scarcely incline a person to pamper himself with luxuries, it seems. Indeed, it should prevent his enjoying himself at all, we are told: "When a man sorroweth perfectly for his sins then all wordly comforts be painful to him. A good man findeth always matter enough why he ought rightfully to sorrow. . . . And the more throughly he considereth himself, the more sorrow he hath."[8]

So those who understood themselves would not naturally make merry; instead, their inclination would be to punish themselves, it seems, to be positively hard on themselves. This is no matter of simply giving up bonbons or beach vacations, either: "When we renounce the superfluous, it is not penance, but temperance: penance is when we give up what is fitting, and the more and more we do this, the greater and better the penance, provided only the subject be not injured or notable infirmity result."[9] There is specific advice for chastising the flesh, so as to suffer the pain we deserve without doing ourselves permanent injury (the trick is to use "thin cords").[10]

To summarize this by saying that self-knowledge would incline one to live a simple life would be an understatement. The idea is that we would be positively hard on ourselves, if we understood what we were like and our place in creation and lived accordingly. Other elements of the tradition counsel similarly. For example, Aquinas warns that what he calls "earthly things" have the power to enthrall us, drawing us away from the contemplative and worshipful life we ought to lead, and thus are better put aside.[11] Ignatius Loyola puts it more powerfully, as usual: I should "ask for understanding of the world, so that I may hate it, and put away from me worldly and vain things."[12]

The life we ought to lead, on this view, is to praise, reverence, and serve God. We need very little by way of material goods in order to manage this. We would know as much, if we understood ourselves and our place in the scheme of things, and we would do our best to stop even *wanting* more than the minimum. One further connection is made between humility and simplicity, on this view, through the fact that Jesus Christ lived simply. Since we are to model ourselves after Jesus, rather than pridefully seeking to live in some different way of our own design, we are to live simply as well.

In sum, there are several ways in which this tradition teaches that the perspective of humility would incline one to abjure material goods except for the barest necessities. Moreover, we commonly associate humility with Christianity: to say that humility is "a Christian virtue" is almost a cliché. Even though Christianity is broader than Catholicism, still we have here an almost univocal authority telling us what it is that Christians value, when they value this virtue that is their specialty. It would be perfectly natural for us to accept unthinkingly its associations between a humble life and an impoverished one.

Humility is one thing, however, and Catholic metaphysics is another. Humility is (very roughly) understanding that we are not any better than we are. Catholic metaphysics is, in part, one account of what it is we would understand, if we understood this. It could be that Catholic metaphysics is correct: that nothing is to our personal credit and we are all to blame for a great deal, that the material world is one temptation after another, and so on. Then, it is certainly arguable, someone who understood himself and his place in the larger scheme of things would want to chastise himself and to avoid the pleasures of the material world as thoroughly as he could.

It could also be, however, that this metaphysics is mistaken, so that the perspective of humility would show us something quite different. The point is that the implications of understanding oneself and one's place depend on what one is like and what one's "place" actually is. Catholic metaphysics is one account of that, but not necessarily the true one. Perhaps instead, as many of us believe, some of our good deeds are our own doing, and some of our virtues are to some extent of our own making. It could be that some of us do have things of which we can properly be proud, in short. It could also be that taking pleasure in material goods is not inherently wicked, and that single-minded worshipfulness is not the sole proper life for us.

No one will expect next a proof of which metaphysical picture is the right one—least of all in a book about humility. Something less ambitious can be undertaken, though. We have seen the case for saying that humility leads to a simple life, on the Catholic view of things. Now let us consider whether the secular, "free will" metaphysics has these same implications.

Let us abandon the Catholic picture of the universe for this other one, and see whether we should still think that a humble person would be inclined to live a simple life.

2

The conception of a simple life to be employed in this exploration is rather imprecise. Roughly speaking, a life is simple to the extent that it tends toward a cot rather than a canopied featherbed, toward clothing for warmth rather than for fashion, toward food for nourishment rather than taste, and so on. The general theme is to keep possessions to a minimum and to keep them starkly functional. The simplicity of a life is thus a matter of degree. The question is whether humility would incline one toward the simpler end of the scale.

A first observation worth making is that some of the more luxurious lives are also throughly self-absorbed. It is possible to spend all one has (and more) on products and services devoted to the appearance of one's face and hair, on food and drink for one's own consumption, and on one's own entertainment and recreation. To do so is to act as if these were the only matters of importance. That is certainly to overestimate them. It is a fascination with oneself that is incompatible with humility: a humble person would know there were other matters of greater importance, as this person does not.

There is, then, at least one sort of very lavish life that humility would strongly disincline a person to lead. Here is an argument with a sterner conclusion. Suppose Robin is aware that there are people who are perishing for want of the very necessities of life, and that he could rescue some of these people from their misery. But Robin spends the money on himself instead, not to buy a fabulous wardrobe, but to bring just a little variety into his daily apparel. This is still to act as if his well-being were more important intrinsically than theirs, the argument goes, since he chooses a small increment for himself over an enormous one for them. In fact, his own well-being does *not* have greater importance: from a neutral point of view, no one is more important intrinsically than anyone else. So, even Robin's behavior is a failure of humility.

The more general message is that a humble person would not provide himself more than the necessities because, as we all know, there are others in the world who are truly miserable. The suggestion is not just that the humble person would live simply in some sanctimonious gesture of solidarity with the wretched of the earth, but that to save others misery he would contribute what he would otherwise have spent on himself.

How far the humble person will go in this direction has been left a bit vague. Perhaps it is as Peter Singer would suggest: a matter of enduring every sacrifice that prevents very bad things from befalling others without imposing similar misery on oneself (or, on still others). That appears to be the way to achieve the neutrality across individuals that the argument suggests will be the humble person's natural bent.

Of course, this is very demanding. It is not just those things we consider luxuries that represent money better spent on someone else. So too does a fair portion of what we would term necessities. For you or me to go without several meals a week would hardly cost us as dearly as it would help the truly destitute to have those same meals. Even allowing for administrative costs, we are headed for the conclusion that humility calls for paring our lives down much closer to the essentials.

The argument to this conclusion is flawed, however. It turns on the claim that a person who buys for herself rather than for those who would benefit more is taking herself to be of greater intrinsic importance than they. That is just the kind of behavior hers is, according to the argument—which is why it would repel any person of humility.

But why is this the proper analysis? No doubt a person *could* be doing exactly this, but could she not also be enacting a broad ethical theory that takes her *not* to be someone inherently special but only to be someone fortunate enough to have the higher cards? Specifically, imagine a person who takes the right of property owners to spend their resources as they wish to be more important than the claim of sufferers not to endure their misery. She might be wrong to do so, of course, but if so she is making an error of ethical theory—not one of attributing greater intrinsic worth to herself. To say that the humble person has a good sense of her own worth does not mean she must have an especially good sense of how utility is to be weighed against liberty.

Nor is the ethical theory we are imagining her holding unhumble itself in some way—unlike, say, the theory that it is her moral duty to take any desire of hers more seriously than any desire of anyone else. To say someone's behavior is not unhumble but merely expresses *that* ethical theory would be unconvincing, because that is a theory only an unhumble person would hold. So, behavior expressing it would turn out to lack humility anyway. The same cannot be said for the view that property rights are more important than life and death: that is not a theory that simply incorporates the unhumility of those who hold it. So, to say our woman is not unhumble but only enacting this ethical view is not a cheap dodge but a genuine alternative.

The upshot is that it is not necessarily arrogant to fail to live the Singerian life. Although others do live in misery, it does not follow that humility must incline one to live very simply and devote one's larger income to relieving that misery. It might so incline one, but it need not.

On the other hand, there is reason to expect that a humble person will not live a lavish life of a certain kind, because this life is so thoroughly self-absorbed. Here, there is an assumption that this particular person is the sole thing of importance: something a person of any humility would know better than to assume.

3

Consider next the Amish, a people who strictly enforce a simple way of life. On pain of exclusion from their community, members are expected to keep to farming occupations whenever possible, to dress as everyone else does, to avoid personal ornamentation, and to live without such modern conveniences as electricity, automobiles, and the telephone. For many reasons, the Amish consider it humble to live this life and prideful to make things easier for oneself.

> When things become too practical and handy, they border on luxury. . . . Sacrifice is a sign of the [properly] yielded self, but luxury signals pride. No longer content to work and sacrifice for the common good, the pleasure-seeker is preoccupied with self-fulfillment. . . . The [properly] yielded self does not seek pleasure, buy luxuries, make things too handy, or pay for "looks."[13]

Some of the Amish reasons for considering humility to require simplicity do not apply to us. For example, it is plausible to hold that to insist on making things easier for oneself while remaining in the Amish community would put the entire way of life at risk. That would be arrogant, it might be argued, a way of acting as if minor improvements in one's lot were more important than enormous disruption for others. A properly humble person would sacrifice those personal advantages for the collective good, the contention would be.[14]

However sound this argument is for the Amish, though, it has no force for us at all. We would not be putting a communal way of life at risk if we were to make things easier for ourselves. Our community has already disintegrated in the way the Amish fear that theirs will. Hence, we can hardly be charged with risking that disintegration for our own petty gain.

An argument with a better chance of surviving transplantation from Amish soil is that acquiring more than the minimal goods represents personal ambition. It involves wanting to do well *for oneself.* Someone could say that it was for the betterment of the community or the glory of God that he obtained his array of fine clothing, fabulous dwellings, incredible automobiles, and so on, but only modern television evangelists seem to be able to say this with a straight face. Even lesser luxuries are things we want for *ourselves,* surely. That shift of focus is enough to render the behavior lacking in humility, on the Amish way of looking at things.[15]

Do those of us who are not Amish also have reason to think that a person of humility would have very little ambition? If so, that is also a reason to expect the humble to live more or less from day to day, marking time and needing little with which to mark it, and thus not collecting the trappings of success. Similarly, we would not expect a person who lacked ambition somehow to do well accidentally, as it were: unless you inherit wealth, we think you have to work hard to have a life of any luxury. If humility does undercut ambition, then, it seems thereby to commit the humble person to a life of relative simplicity.

But, does humility undercut ambition? It probably would if to be humble were to have a low opinion of oneself. For, if you thought yourself short on ability, you would consider any great accomplishments to be reserved for others, it seems. It is so customary to equate humility with low self-esteem that this alone might explain why we might expect humility to sap ambition. I have argued strenuously that the equation is mistaken, however. Is there any other basis for the expectation?

One candidate runs as follows. Suppose that to be humble is to have your talents and accomplishments in proper perspective, just as I have argued. Would that perspective not show you just how trivial anything you could ever do would be? You would see it against the vastness of the universe, after all, against the billions who came before you, the billions who exist at the same time as you, and the billions who are to come. No image of a teeming anthill or a great beach composed of billions of grains of sand would capture quite how momentary you are, and how less than momentary anything you did would be. Your greatest accomplishment would be as close to nothing as to make no matter.

What would understanding that do to ambition? The argument is that only those who fail to understand it are driven to attempt "great things." Such people foolishly think their success would be more than the mark a single grain of sand might leave in an endless sandstorm. The humble know better. They are not ambitious, not because they do not think they can do as well as others can, but because they know that nothing anyone does really amounts to anything. They know nothing they would do is worth any great effort to do it; they have the wisdom of humility, and they escape thereby the foolishness of ambition.

Now, there is no doubt that contemplating the vastness of the universe can induce a mood of futility. Perhaps that mood inspired the memorable poetry about Ozymandias, king of kings, who seems so plainly wrong about the greatness of his achievements. The argument I have set out claims to do more than express a mood, however. Specifically, it claims that a humble person would understand that nothing she could do would be worth a great effort, and that she would therefore spend herself less ambitiously. But is this not to regard great effort by her as a thing of value—a thing that is therefore misspent if it does not purchase a great achievement? If only great accomplishments would be worthy recompense for great effort, then great effort must itself be a thing of considerable importance.

That is a possible view. It takes us to be in the *wrong place*, so to speak, where there is nothing worthy of our spending this valuable coin. It concludes that we would be wiser to hold the coin in reserve. (For what, exactly, is not said.) That is an impressive pessimism about the world, but it is not humility.

Nor is it a natural part of seeing oneself as a single speck of sand, interestingly enough. To see yourself as insignificant would be to see neither your accomplishments *nor your efforts* as having any importance: on a cosmic scale the efforts are no more substantial, surely, but just as momentary and puny. If that were your view, you would feel no incongruity between spending your efforts and accomplishing only something quite small. Instead, you would consider it perfectly suitable that something so trivial as your efforts would achieve something so trivial as your potential accomplishments.

In short, the perspective of humility does not sap ambition by bringing home one's cosmic insignificance. It does not show that trying very hard to do something is somehow profligate, though it does teach various other lessons. Perhaps it teaches that there are limits to how proud one should be of anything one achieved and that there are limits to the level of achievement to which one should aspire. Transgressing those limits would be a way of taking oneself too seriously—as, ironically, would be the idea that only a timeless, magnificent accomplishment would merit your working very hard at anything.

A quite different line of thought about ambition is that what an ambitious person really wants is recognition. He wants to "make a name for himself," as the Amish put it: he wants standing in the eyes of others, just as (Aquinas observed) at least part of what an envious person fears is that he will lose that standing once others see how someone has surpassed him.[16] If recognition *is* the true aim of ambition, it might seem again that a humble person would not be ambitious: there is something a little incongruous about a humble person thirsting after fame.

Against this, however, it must be noted that it is not at all clear that every ambition does involve a desire for fame or recognition. It appears to be perfectly possible to be ambitious about tasks one just considers challenging for their own sake, rather than for any fame they might bring. Your ambition could be just to solve some fascinating problem, for example, regardless of whether this ever comes to light. Since those are ambitions a humble person could have without also thirsting for fame, the argument cannot show that a humble person must lack ambition.

There is no doubt that some ambitions do reflect an exaggerated conception of oneself. Presumably, a humble person would not be given to those ambitions, since his humility would acquaint him with his limitations. Notice also, though, that no one is perfectly acquainted with his limitations, nor is it always obvious what capacities a particular task would require. So there can be a lack of humility in being utterly certain that something is beyond you, an improper confidence in your grasp of your capabilities and of the task at hand.

In other words, humility actually requires being somewhat open to possibilities. Admittedly, that is not the same as having ambitions: to have an ambition is to want something and to set at least some thoughts if not some efforts toward obtaining it. Still, humility gives ambition a place to grow: just the opposite of the thought that it must choke ambition off at the root, and restrict one thereby to a simple life.

4

A different question is whether humility might call for simplicity because the alternative is to live too ostentatiously. As Thomas Aquinas put it, "Excess in outward expenditure and parade is wont to be done with a view toward boasting, which is supressed by humility. Accordingly humility has to do, in a secondary way, with externals."[17] Some years ago, the popular press commonly used the phrase "conspicuous consumption" to refer to a pattern of purchases so ostentatiously expensive as to demand our attention. The phenomenon of conspicuous consumption is still with us, surely, but the phrase seems to have disappeared. Perhaps we no longer think of conspicuous consumption as a bad thing, which was the implication of the phrase. At any rate, it is something to which there is a certain knack, since not every incredibly expensive item screams "This was incredibly expensive!" nor are all of them suffi-cently suited to the "parading," which is vital to consuming conspicuously. Those who manage conspicuous consumption are evidently not living the spare and simple life. Is there rea-son to think that theirs is not a life a humble person would adopt?

Aquinas thought so. The reason he offers is that the per-son who lives this way is probably boasting, that humility "suppresses" boasting, and thus that it "suppresses" this way of life. This argument is worth a closer look. There is little doubt that typically the point of conspicuous consumption is to be conspicuous: to capture our attention, that is. Someone might have some other reason for owning an automobile that the rest of us could buy only if we sold our houses and moved into it, but we are thinking here of a person who has a great many possessions like this; someone who "parades" his wealth. The longer and gaudier the parade, the stronger the suspicion that its point is to impress us. We can come to be reasonably confident that he buys and displays these things so that we will be forced to see how very well he is doing.

Does that make conspicuous consumption a way of boast-ing? If we think first of verbal boasting, we may notice that it sometimes involves exaggeration, or even outright lying. Very often, the story the boaster tells puts him a bit more at the center of things than he actually was, or makes what he did more difficult or its reception more appreciative, and so on.

Still, the tendency to embellish does not seem to be the essence of boasting; it seems instead to be a side effect of the fact that someone who boasts wants to impress. After all, it also seems possible to boast without misdescribing what one did. To wish that someone would not boast is not just to wish that he would stick to the facts. It is to wish that he would not crow and strut, that he would not go *on* so about it (or, perhaps, that he would not tell us about it yet again). In the same way, if we urge our children not to boast about their report cards, we do not mean merely that they should not lie and say they got straight As. We mean something a bit more subtle, about not demanding that others pay more attention to what they have done than their accomplishments merit.

What a boastful person does is to seek to draw attention to herself by mentioning some achievement, possession, important friend, and so on, when this is inappropriate in some way. (If it were *not* inappropriate she would not be boasting, it seems to me, but only providing relevant information.) What makes the boastful remark inappropriate varies considerably. Perhaps it is someone else's moment in the sun, but this person pushes forward to tell us about herself. Perhaps we simply have other topics of conversation under way, but she interrupts to redirect our attention to her own favorite subject. Perhaps her stories are tiresomely familiar and have long since gained her whatever applause from us they merit. The point of a boast is always to impress, and the timing is always bad.

All of this is good news for the view that conspicuous consumption is typically a way of boasting. For, when someone's purchases scream that he is making money hand over fist, they may be perfectly truthful: he *is* making money hand over fist. Thus, if a remark could not be a boast unless it were untrue, the suitably wealthy person would not be boasting by living this way. But if (as suggested) a boast is an inappropriate effort to impress by saying something favorable about oneself, then conspicuous consumption might very well turn out to be boasting after all. For, the point of conspicuous consumption is to impress, we have said, and it represents a more or less constant effort to do so: the lavish purchases are steadily on parade, and so reek of wealth as to be hard to ignore.

Living this way does not seem much different from regaling people with one *story* after another about how well one is doing.

Arguably, then, conspicuous consumption is a way of boasting. According to Aquinas, this means it would go against a humble person's nature, because boasting is unhumble. He was right: it does.[18] To boast is to demand more attention to your good deeds, stellar traits, and so on than these are due. A person might do this in the false belief that he *was* due our attention, that we were *wrong* not to find him riveting and not to want to marvel over what he had done. Humility would work against that sort of boasting, since it works against false beliefs of this kind.

Nor would a humble person be inclined to boast willfully, knowing perfectly well that she did not deserve the attention she sought but hoping to get it anyway. To do this would be to act as if her getting the attention were the thing of primary importance: more important, for example, than the attention remaining on someone who actually did deserve it. That would be to overstep herself, in a way thoroughly unappealing to a person of humility. Keep in mind, too, that the boasting done by a life of conspicuous consumption is not a matter of succumbing to an occasional temptation to boast, as even a humble person might. It is to make the broadcast at every opportunity.

Insofar as a lavish life is boastful, then, we have good reason to think that a humble person would not live it. The same would apply to someone who lived this way not merely to brag about how well she was doing but in hopes of making others envious, of making them "eat their hearts out." Her project would be to make others feel like failures by forcing them to see how fabulously well she was doing. If trying to force her success upon their attention is unhumble, doing so to make them envious would be as well, certainly.

It is also possible to live lavishly without doing so either to impress or to foment envy, however. For example, someone could live this way because he had great wealth, no thrift, and absolutely no taste. Then many of his purchases would seem to us to have nothing to recommend them except that they cost a great deal to make. So we might come to think of him as seeking our attention—when actually he had no interest in it at all. Someone else might want the top of the line in all things just because that pleased her or was her personal way of rewarding or motivating herself, or because it reassured her (rightly or wrongly) of her personal worth. Since none of these people would be living lavishly as a way of boasting, to show that boasting is unhumble is not to show that living lavishly is unhumble.

All these lives would in fact draw attention to a person, however, despite not being designed to do so. Living unusually well just does make one a subject of interest to others, regardless of one's intentions. In the next section I consider whether that makes it something a humble person would prefer not to do.

5

The size and number of mirrors in a society indicate the cultural importance attached to the self. Thus it is not surprising that the mirrors found in Amish houses are smaller and fewer than those found in modern ones. Whereas Moderns are preoccupied with "finding themselves," the Amish are engaged in "losing themselves." The Amish work just as hard at losing themselves as Moderns work at finding themselves.[19]

Two things about the Amish are likely to strike us "Moderns" rather forcefully: their rejection of most technology, and the degree to which they blend into a mass rather than standing out as individuals. They dress alike, and rather drably at that. Their buggies are all the same boxy shape and are either gray or black. Since there are few great differences in how well anyone is doing and only certain forms of technology are permitted, individuals tend to have the same things along other lines as well.

The uniformity is not absolute.[20] Still, the idea is to blend in and disappear, rather than to stand out and be recognized. The desired way of life "entails a modest way of acting, talking, dressing, and walking."[21] A properly socialized Amish person wants not to stand out but to be unremarkable: "Modern culture produces individualists whose prime objective is personal fulfillment. By contrast, the goal of Gelassenheit is a subdued, humble person who discovers fulfillment in the community. Amish who give up their selves to the community receive, in return, a durable and visible ethnic identity."[22] Should we have something of this in our own conception of what it is to be humble? Should we think of the humble person as preferring to live quietly, that is, as being uncomfortable when he comes to the attention of others?

We can start our thinking about this by borrowing a distinction the Amish evidently make themselves about who takes notice of one. To quote Donald Kraybill again, "The Amish deplore public recognition, but in face-to-face conversation there are many warm moments of recognition and gentle praise for personal contributions."[23] For your acts to come to the notice of those whom they directly affect is inevitable, and there is nothing wrong, on this view, with their praising you for what you have done. But why would anything you had done call for similar acknowledgment from total strangers, with whom your actions had nothing to do?

Perhaps if the strangers were to learn of what you had done, it would follow that they ought to be impressed, that they ought to feel a neutral moral admiration. That might follow if what you had done was a very good thing. To say the deed must be *brought to their notice* is to make a much stronger claim about it, however. There is no reason to think that very much of what a person does is this significant: certainly not, for example, the fact that he is doing very well financially. That is of importance to those it affects, but not to those it does not.

Accordingly, there would be something wrong with living in a way that broadcast that you were doing very well, even if you did not mean it as a boast. You would be acting as if your flourishing were so noteworthy an event that it justified interrupting the lives of strangers to so inform them. A person who had the matter in proper perspective would be inclined to keep his prosperity more to himself, the argument runs.

This is not an argument for a simple life, however; it is an argument for an unobstrusive life, which is not quite the same thing. The argument says a humble person would be disposed to adopt a sort of protective coloration, so that others might get on with their lives. That would certainly mean a simple life if all about you were living simply. But, suppose they were not? Then to insist on a cabin, a pallet, and thin gruel would hardly be inconspicuous. It might even be a way of boasting about one's virtuous asceticism.

Still, if the argument is sound, it retains this much force: humility would incline a person to limit his comforts so that he did not live in a strikingly lavish way. That is far from saying it would incline him to chastise his flesh, but not far from the conclusions of some other arguments we have considered: that a humble person would not live in a wholly self-absorbed way, or in a way designed to boast of his accomplishments.

A further question about the current argument is whether reluctance to come to public notice is a feature of humility, or actually of something else that we are confusing with humility: shyness, for example, or modesty. Being shy certainly involves a tendency to be embarrassed by attention, public or otherwise. So, part of a shy person's personality would be a disinclination to live in a way such that strangers were bound to take notice. It would not follow, however, that a humble person would have this same disinclination, because being shy and being humble are two different things.

The same applies to modesty. To be modest, it seems, is to be reticent about presenting what you take to be your good points. A modest person would prefer not to talk about what she did, would prefer not to put herself forward. Her reluctance does not involve a lack of self-confidence, as the shy person's does. Thus it does not involve being uncomfortable whenever all eyes turn to her, as the shy person is, but only when called upon to say something good about herself. She too would be uncomfortable about living in a noticeably wealthy way, insofar as this amounted to putting herself forward. But, again, for modesty to have this implication is not for humility to have it, because modesty and humility are two different things.

All of this is true enough, it seems to me, but also inconclusive. It is true that modest and shy persons would be reluctant to live ostentatiously, and also that humility is not the same as modesty or shyness. It remains possible that humility *also* involves this reluctance, however, in a different way of its own.

For example, a shy person would be reluctant to live ostentatiously for the same reason she would not wish to speak in public: because being noticed is a painful thing for her. According to our original argument, it is not "being noticed" that would disturb the person of humility, though. It is the fact that his own behavior exaggerates the importance of what he has done, presses him upon strangers. So the argument does not confuse humility with shyness; it maintains that, whatever is true of shy people, humble people are disinclined to be pushy.

Similarly, what puts modest people off is not putting themselves forward for attention they do not deserve. It is putting themselves forward at all. Whether they merit favorable attention is irrelevant: they just do not like the idea of claiming the praise. That is a broader feature than the humble person's reluctance to press beyond his due. Both the humble and the modest person might oppose living in ways that called public attention to the fact that they were flourishing: the modest person because this amounted to tooting his own horn, the humble one, I have argued, because this was the wrong time to toot it.

We would be wrong to think this last argument confuses humility with shyness or with modesty. It offers, instead, an independent reason for believing that humility would dispose a person not to live so blatantly well as to press his personal success upon the notice of strangers. That is not a basis for expecting that a humble person must live ascetically, but it is a reason not to expect to find a humble person in a palace.

6

That turns out to be the most we can say about humility and the simple life, assuming we do not accept the direct connection offered by Aquinas, Ignatius Loyola, Thomas à Kempis, Bernard of Clairvaux, and the other fathers of the church. A humble person will not be thoroughly self-absorbed, but this does not mean she must give up her substance for the good of others. A humble person will not have certain exaggerated ambitions, but this does not mean she will so lack ambition that a simple life will suit her fine and will be all she can hope to achieve. A humble person will not live boastfully or in hopes of making others envious, but this allows for creature comforts well beyond the minimal. A humble person will be disinclined to live opulently, but being disinclined to live opulently is not the same as being inclined to make one's life intentionally hard or unencumbered by goods beyond the barest necessities.

8

THE
VIRTUE
OF
HUMILITY

A recurrent theme of this book is that humility is not what it is often taken to be. Humility is not a meek lack of self-respect or low self-esteem or the undervaluing of one's good qualities. If it were any of these, then to be humble would be pitiable at best. There is an element of resignation in the attitudes mentioned, a hopelessness so resistant to encouragement as eventually to try the most sympathetic patience. Such an outlook should be no one's ideal, surely.

A different complaint about humility construed in these ways is that it would often embody a mistake. Anyone who undervalues his good qualities is thereby wrong about them; no one should lack self-respect; and, although there are people whose low opinion of themselves would be accurate enough, there are also a great many for whom a low opinion would be quite mistaken. Hence, a humble attitude would embody an error about oneself if it were the attitude described. That makes it hard, once again, to see why anyone should value humility: why should it be virtuous to have a false view of yourself?

Finally, consider for a moment the person of great accomplishment or great virtue who has retained her humility, despite the over-excited praise of others. Hers is the kind of humility we most admire, having come to expect heroes to be a bit full of themselves instead. But if humility consists in thinking one amounts to very little, has done nothing, and so on, it does not even seem possible for these heroes to be humble. We lesser types know that this is not the truth about them; surely they would know it too? Surely they could not fail to notice that they were very good people, or that they had done something of great difficulty or great benefit to mankind, or whatever. So their humility would have to be *false* humility, then; it would have to be that annoying pretense that spoils our pleasure in contemplating someone excellent and dampens our admiration for him.

In short, this conception of humility is difficult to retain if we believe that there are good and accomplished people in the world and that such people are capable of humility. It is impossible to retain if, as we think, their humility is especially admirable. Finally, it makes very puzzling the high esteem in which humility is commonly held. Why so many of us consider it a virtue at all is hard to see, if being humble amounts to lacking self-respect or undervaluing one's good qualities or having a low opinion of oneself that is somehow more praiseworthy the more mistaken it is.

I have offered a different analysis, according to which humility consists, roughly, in having oneself and one's accomplishments in perspective. On this view, to be humble is to understand yourself and your moral entitlements sufficiently clearly that you are disposed not to exaggerate about these. How *that* could be a good thing in a person is not puzzling, I take it; nor is our admiration for it. It does not seem impossible, either, for an especially accomplished person to retain this perspective (unlike his holding the clearly false belief that he had done very little). It seems only a *difficult* thing to do: which, in turn, explains why humility might be especially admirable in such a person. In sum, humility is no longer paradoxical in the ways mentioned, if we construe it as suggested.

What would it be like to have this unexaggerated perspective on yourself and what you had done? In part, it would involve understanding certain facts about yourself. You would be realistic about your abilities and your limitations, rather than thinking yourself abler than you were. Similarly, you would understand rightly the things you had accomplished, rather than believing them to have been more difficult or more nobly motivated or more far reaching in their consequences than they actually were. You would not exaggerate the part that (as a matter of fact) you play in the lives of others. You would not overestimate the contributions you had made to their achievements or the extent to which what they did was meant to affect you (as opposed to affecting you only in passing) or the extent to which you were in competition with them.

Getting these facts straight is one part of what it is to be humble. What humility works against is not simply thinking of the facts about you as *different* from what they are but thinking of them as *better*. Humility works against believing yourself more able than you actually are, for example, thinking you can accomplish things that are well beyond your reach. Humility also works against overestimating yourself morally: against believing that you merit more praise and gratitude than you actually do, for example, or considering yourself entitled to behave in ways in which you are not. Those are flattering pictures of oneself, but false ones; a humble person grasps the truth sufficiently clearly to resist them.

Humility also provides an understanding that one is not special, from the point of view of the universe, not an exception to be treated differently from the others. "Of course I'm not an exception," we may be inclined to think, "only an utter loon would believe himself the universe's chosen child." But, in fact, the mistake is much more common: it occurs whenever we expect mistreatment and misfortune to bo takcn more seriously when they happen to us than we would think appropriate when they happen to others. The mistake occurs, too, whenever someone acts as if she may do things that others in similar situations may not do. For, these are ways of taking oneself to be exceptional, and they are hardly rare.

So humility protects us from a mistake life offers us many opportunities to make. To say more specifically how it affords this protection describes what it is to be humble. Now to pull together some elements of that description.

1

No one is always treated exactly as he or she should be. The luckiest do not suffer deeds of great violence or wrenching betrayals or smothering subjugation, but even the luckiest sometimes find that they have been cheated or deceived or treated unjustly. How would humility incline a person to respond to whatever mistreatment came his way? Would it dispose him not to take offense, for example? And, if he did take offense, would it make him hasten to extend forgiveness to the wrongdoer?

So it might appear, and this seems to some to render humility indistinguishable from a lack of self-respect. For the most part, however, self-respect requires only that we not demote ourselves beneath the class in which we place others. Humility would certainly not foster such a demotion. Instead it would foster the reverse: understanding yourself and your accomplishments should incline you to recognize that you are certainly not some lesser being who must accept mistreatment as your due.

While humility therefore does not require a meek submissiveness, as noted, it does require that we take whatever happens to us to be no more important intrinsically than it would be if it befell another. Your being shortchanged at the store calls for no stronger reaction than would anyone else's being shortchanged: no stronger reaction, that is, from the victim, from strangers, from those who penalize wrongdoers, from the wrongdoer himself. So, the properly humble attitude is to be no more resentful than you would consider it appropriate for anyone to be, and not to expect any more sympathy or support or remorse from the others, either.

This view permits the humble person to be resentful, of course, and to withhold forgiveness, unlike the view that we must never take offense and must always forgive. There is no self-elevation in taking offense, as long as we are consistent. Nor is there any in being unforgiving, as long as we regard that as a suitable attitude for any victim of the same mistreatment. It is essential that this consistency hold across cases in which we are the wrongdoer rather than the victim: we must take the wrong equally seriously then, if we are not to be taking ourselves too seriously. When we do not, our attitude is that what happens to us has a unique importance to it, however blind others might be to this fact.

We lack humility in a different fashion when we take what is really only indifference to our interests to be something more focused on us. A good deal of mistreatment is like that, I believe. It involves no intention to do us harm, that is, but only a certain lack of interest in how we might be affected. To think there is more to an episode than that is to overestimate your centrality to the great flow of events: a mistake against which humility provides protection.

2

Another fact of life is that there are people in great misery in the world because of natural disasters and the like. We could help them, and we know it. Mostly we do not do so, though, but go about our own lives. What does humility require of a person here?

A thesis modeled on Peter Singer's work would be that not to be greatly alive to the needs of others is a failure of humility.[1] Specifically, we should be moved to sacrifice anything to help them, up to the point of doing comparable harm in making the sacrifice. On this view, to fall short of such sacrifice is to act as if lesser benefits to ourselves were more important than greater benefits to others: as if our having a new suit or a weekend at the beach were more important than several other human beings' being rescued from miserable starvation. That would be to act as if we were more important than they, the argument continues: since we are not, this is a failure of moral humility on our part.

I have argued instead that humility requires two things of us in our compassion for those in distress: consistency like that required in our reactions to wrongdoing and avoidance of self-absorption. To be consistent we need not be as upset over the plight of those in distress as we would be if it were our own (or as upset as if it were the plight of "a neighbor's child ten yards from me," in Singer's phrase), any more than we need be as outraged over their being assaulted as we would be if we were assaulted ourselves. What is necessary instead is that we not take distress to be any more significant intrinsically because it is we who suffer it, just as a moral wrong is not any more significant intrinsically because we are its victim. Most of us take our being in even *minor* trouble to be something strangers should take very seriously. So, humility requires most of us to take the *major* troubles of strangers very seriously. Our usual indifference to them is a failure of moral humility.

Humility demands as well that we avoid self-absorption. To call someone self-absorbed is to say she is fascinated by such matters as her own appearance, her image, her personality or character, her progress up life's ladder, her evening's entertainment, and so on. What fascinates the self-absorbed person is herself; to say she is *fascinated* means that she is very difficult to distract from attending to herself, in the same way as a child absorbed in a game is difficult to draw away into other pursuits. There is a level of self-absorption that amounts to taking oneself too seriously, relative to other matters. To do so is to exaggerate one's own importance, and therefore to lack humility.

Which failures to respond compassionately would qualify as unhumbly self-absorbed? The clearest examples verge on the pathological: Singer's man who would let a child drown rather than muddy his clothes, James Rachels's diners who would let a child starve at their feet rather than interrupt their repast. The underlying idea is one of being undiverted from self-centered pursuits even when the calls to compassion are loud and clear. What makes a call to compassion "loud and clear" is a complicated matter of human psychology, but some of its elements seem identifiable, along the following lines.

Generally, suffering in one's presence is more vivid than suffering that is only described, and the suffering of someone who has been a part of your life is more vivid to you than the suffering of some imagined member of a future generation. Even the most wrenching agony can fail to grip us if it is described only statistically, and something much less serious can be depicted far more compellingly by focusing our attention on some particular waif. There may also be a loss of vividness when the call on our compassion is one among many, rather than one standing alone in stark contrast.

No doubt, there is much more to all this. The main point here is that whatever the particulars turn out to be, for a person to be undistracted from self-centered pursuits by even the more vivid and desparate calls on her compassion is for her to take herself too seriously. That is a moral mistake a humble person would not make.

3

Although the world contains many who are far worse off than we, it also contains many who are far better off. And not only wealthier than we, of course: there are plenty who are better philosophers, plenty who are nicer people, and Lord *knows* there are plenty who are better looking. What is more, others sometimes get the recognition we would like to have, or the respect, or the affection.

This means there are many occasions for bitterness: for feeling unjustly treated by life or injured by a rival or envious or jealous of those who are doing better. It is possible to admire those who surpass you instead, or, at least, to take their superiority in stride. Nearly all of us are capable of these nobler-sounding reactions at times. For someone *always* to be so mature when surpassed would seem almost inhuman, however. How would humility dispose a person toward those who seem to put him in the shade?

Notice here how often the hard feelings we have on these occasions are unreasonable, in one way or another. It is not as if those who surpass us were to blame for our relative positions, as if they had held us back while they surged ahead, and might sensibly be resented as people who had done us wrong. Nor are we always realistic when our envy passes quickly into complaints about injustice, as if the gap between us were due to some unfair third party who has not taken our merit properly into account. These reactions evince a certain unwillingness to believe the truth about oneself, an inclination to substitute some grander person who is never surpassed except through chicanery. A humble person would know herself better than that, and thus her humility would protect her against hard feelings that are unreasonable in this way.

Similarly, both jealousy and envy can be imbued with a lack of realism about one's possibilities. Thus, some are greatly upset when surpassed by individuals against whom they quite wrongly suppose they should be able to compete on equal terms. If they knew themselves better, they would not take these to be failures that call for self-reproach, or for special explanations preserving the false picture of themselves. Yet another element of understanding oneself is to be realistic about one's place in the lives of others, rather than presuming there to be commitments and relationships of intimacy when none is present. That spares a person the jealous rages and hurt feelings of those who feel betrayed, despite not being entitled to any such feelings.

Even when hard feelings are appropriate, there is still a matter of keeping them in proportion, moreover, and here too humility comes into play: overreacting to defeat or to displacement is a failure of humility. Suppose that whatever else we have been to each other, I now think of you mainly, if not exclusively, as the person who received the bigger raise or confided in someone else rather than in me, and this puts a distance and reserve between us. Clearly, this can exaggerate the importance of these things happening to me, taking them to be far more significant events in the history of the universe than they are. Clearly too, it may be that I would consider this reaction excessive if someone else were to carry on in the same way. Humility inclines us not to elevate ourselves in either of these ways.

One further benefit of humility is an understanding that you are not in nearly so many competitions as those prone to envy seem to think they are in. Ordinarily, the success of another person does not put you behind in a race in the way the envious person takes it to. Ordinarily, their success has nothing to do with you at all. Similarly, the fact that someone else is wonderful in some way does not ordinarily mean that you are losing in some cosmic competition for best in show. This false picture of the world sees many connections between you and others that are simply not there: as if there were a web connecting you with them, so that any shift in their position had something to do with you. That is a very unhumble picture, surely. Those who view their place in the universe more realistically gain protection from the envy and jealousy that afflict those who consider life a constant competition on multiple fronts.

4

We come next to efforts to influence or control someone's behavior for that person's own good. Such efforts often implement genuine concern for another's well-being and seem to be a normal impulse toward those about whom we care. Notoriously, however, they can also be overbearing and intrusive, regardless of how welcome the feelings behind them might be. Here, too, we can expect a little humility to have some welcome effects. For what is wrong with objectionable efforts to steer us in the right direction is not merely that they often have bad results but that they are arrogant. Our complaint against them is that it is not this person's *place* to act as she has: that she has overestimated herself, or underestimated us, or both.

In some cases what she has done is to overestimate her abilities, taking herself to be equipped to do better by us than we could ourselves, without justification for believing such a thing. In other cases, the mistake is not in her conception of what she is *like* but in her view of what this entitles her to do. She may lack moral humility, that is, in the same way as someone who believes that his charm and wit make him an exception, somehow, to the moral rules which restrict us lesser beings. Whichever sort of arrogance an act of paternalism embodies, we may expect it to repel a person of humility, in the same way as a kind person would be repelled by an element of cruelty in a course of action.

Interestingly, it is not the case that certain strategies are always arrogant and certain others always free of arrogance: for example, that it is always arrogant to use force but never arrogant to use reason. Instead, even so mild a measure as providing information can be arrogant, and even laying hands on someone can be free of arrogance, depending on the circumstances. Accordingly, what the humble person's aversion to arrogance provides is sensitivity to when a measure might be taken and when it would be out of place. It is also arguable that humility would incline a person toward less coercive measures rather than more coercive, other things being equal.

One further point of interest concerning paternalism is that it sometimes seems to make a considerable difference whether the person one is looking after is a friend or a stranger. Behavior that would show affectionate concern toward a friend might be thoroughly objectionable if he were a stranger; behavior showing a perfectly acceptable unconcern for a stranger might be unforgiveable neglect if he were a friend; and so on. An account of these differences can be given in terms of humility and arrogance, for friends typically invite the expression of concern for their well-being. This invitation entitles the other party to act in this way, where a stranger would overstep himself by doing the same. Friends may also make it clear that concern is not only invited but expected and may nurture the belief that this expectation will be fulfilled.

Humility would contribute to a person's sensitivity in such matters. In part, humility would make her disinclined to assume invitations where none has been extended. That would make the humble person less likely to act toward a stranger in ways that should be reserved for the stranger's friends. It would also make the humble person less likely to exceed in unwelcome ways an invitation that has been offered: less likely to go too far in looking after her friends, that is.

In any case, since humility makes a person averse to the presumptuousness of paternalism, a humble person would not aspire to exercise great control over the lives of others for their own good, or envy those who had this kind of power. She would not envy an aging matriarch her continuing ability to mother her grown children, for example, or the power the wealthy sometimes exercise over those willing to live as they are told.[2]

5

So much for the effects of humility on a person's inclination to look after others for their own good. We are also the *object* of such attentions, from time to time. What has humility to do with accepting or rejecting them?

No doubt it should open a person to the possibility that he does not know best, that his information is incomplete or his inferences faulty. No doubt it should mean that efforts to help him will not necessarily fall on deaf ears, that is. But something much more intriguing comes up when we note that people sometimes wish to make their own way, not because they are sure theirs must be the better way, but just for the sake of making their own decisions. There is a declaration of independence in this, a celebration of autonomy. Can it ever be unhumble to make this stand? Is doing so a failure of moral humility, a way of taking oneself to be uniquely important? Or is the thought that one could go too far here left over from confusing humility with meekness and a lack of self-respect?

The answer depends, I think, on what it is for something to be a particular person's life, since this is what grounds that person's interests in shaping it. Once those interests are clear, we can see when insisting these interests be served would be unhumble, and when it would not.

On my view, it is wrong to think of our lives as something we own, or as something given to us or entrusted to our care, or as plays or stories in which we are the main characters. The less colorful truth is that a life is nothing but a series of actions, experiences, and biological processes, given unity by being made up of the actions, experiences, and biological processes of a particular person. For a life to be *your* life is just for you to be the person whose actions (etc.) make it up.

If so, you have several powerful interests in shaping the life as you prefer. For one thing, since you are the one who will have the experiences, you have a corresponding interest in having those experiences be of one kind rather than another. In addition, each stretch of a life happens only once; to lose the chance to shape it as you wish is therefore to lose something irreplaceable.

Moreover, part of understanding yourself is knowing that you are someone who would do this under those circumstances rather than that: understanding yourself is parasitic on understanding your actions. Often, actions are far better understood when they are allowed to occur and to have their ramifications than when they are only contemplated. Accordingly, to have your actions blocked, even "for your own good," is to have your basis for understanding yourself undercut.

In addition, to limit our understanding of who we are also undercuts our basis for thinking well or ill of ourselves. Limiting our understanding of ourselves makes self-esteem and self-criticism that much more dubious. We each have an interest in being right about what our strengths and weaknesses are and in how we add up: to have been foolish about ourselves might amuse an audience of cruel gods but seems a ludicrous way to spend one's only hours on the stage.

These interests in making our own major decisions are joined by a very deep *preference* for making them, on the occasions in question. For, these are times when a person makes a stand for independence, by insisting that it is *his* life that others seek to direct. As a set of interests these are very powerful, more so than virtually anything that the paternalist could offer in support of her contention that it is nevertheless in one's *best* interest to have the decision made differently by someone else. Acordingly, asserting those interests in order to deflect paternalism is well within the limits of humility. One is only insisting on serving one's strongest interests, and there is nothing unhumble about that.

But lives can be so intertwined that a decision cannot shape one life without also shaping another. Then both parties have interests of the same kind, and the possibility arises anew that it could be a failure of humility for one party to insist on having his own way. What is needed is to compare the extent to which a decision shapes one life with the extent to which it shapes another. That provides the sense in which it *can* be claiming more than one's due to insist on shaping one's life as one prefers, without collapsing into a view that humility requires self-abnegation.

6

There are several respects in which we associate humility with living simply, unencumbered by possessions beyond the bare minimum. We expect a humble person to live in a humble dwelling, not in opulence, and to eat humble fare, not rich dishes. Is there anything to this? Would genuine humility incline one to forego whatever is beyond the essentials, so that our own more luxurious lives betray the extent to which we have not achieved it?

That might well be the truth of the matter, if the fathers of the Roman Catholic church were correct in thinking that every good thing about a person is God's gift and every bad one that person's own doing. For, it might well follow that understanding yourself would incline you to make your life as hard as you could manage, in penance for misusing your gifts. And similarly, if not overestimating your place in the larger scheme of things meant realizing that all earthly pleasures are a snare and a delusion, then someone with the right attitude would avoid such pleasures, presumably. In short, if this Catholic metaphysics is correct about what is understood by those who do not overestimate themselves, then such an understanding might very well incline a person to live not merely a simple life but one he or she intentionally made hard.

This may not be the correct metaphysical view, however. The truth may be what many of us believe: that we sometimes deserve credit for the things we do and become, that a life wholly devoted to worship is not the only proper one for us, and that earthly pleasures are not intrinsically wicked. It is interesting to consider what would follow if *that* were the truth of the matter: would a humble perspective still incline a person to live simply?

There are several reasons to think so, I believe, but it is important not to overstate their implications. A humble person will not be thoroughly self-absorbed, but this is far from saying he must give up his substance for the good of others. A humble person will not have certain exaggerated ambitions, but this does not mean he will so lack ambition that a simple life will suit him fine and will be all he can hope to achieve. A humble person will not live boastfully or in hopes of making others envious, but this allows for creature comforts well beyond the minimal. A humble person will be disinclined to live opulently, but this is not the same as being inclined to make one's life intentionally hard or to limit one's goods to the barest necessities.

Just as we might exaggerate the extent to which humility calls for austerity in one's life, we might also exaggerate the extent to which it forbids us to be proud of anything. Richard Taylor does so in the following passage: "Pride is quite correctly perceived to be incompatible with . . . the supposed virtue of humility that is so congenial to the devout mind and so foreign to the pagan temperament."[3] By "the supposed virtue of humility that is so congenial to the devout mind," however, Taylor means the conviction that we are utterly worthless. No doubt that conviction *is* incompatible with being proud of anything, just as he asserts, but, as we have seen, there are good reasons for taking humility to be something else altogether.

On the account offered here, humility does not preclude our taking what is sometimes called proper pride in ourselves and our accomplishments, but only guards against our being foolishly or excessively proud. To say only this much is rather abstract and uniformative, however. It would be nice to have some idea of *when* pride is foolish or excessive, and therefore not the humble person's style, and when it is pride of a kind a humble person might take.

We should start our thoughts about this by considering what pride is. As many have noted, to be proud of something is not the same as simply taking pleasure in it. You might take pleasure in the lovely view from a secluded hillside, for example, taking every opportunity to visit and enjoy it, without being at all *proud* of the view. If you had managed to complete a marathon, on the other hand, you might be not merely pleased by this but also proud of it. The difference lies in your taking completing the marathon to speak well of you, in some way, and *not* thinking of the view from the hillside in those terms. You regard the view only as a pleasure, while you take completing the marathon to be something to your credit.

If this is the correct account of pride, we should be proud of exactly those things that we would be right to regard as to our credit. We would be wrong to be proud of things that do not speak well of us, or that we have insufficient reason to take to do so. And our pride would be excessive, insofar as we drew grander implications than we had grounds to draw. What humility does, in general terms, is to protect us against errors of each kind. Humility inclines us to be proud only of what actually is to our credit and only when we are justified in thinking of it in that way, and it keeps our pride proportionate rather than exaggerated.

To be more specific requires venturing a view about which things actually are to a person's credit. Since that is a very difficult matter, to say precisely how humility would affect pride is difficult. One appropriately cautious hypothesis runs as follows, however.

Notice, first, how very *strange* it would be for you to be proud of the hillside vista, as opposed to simply enjoying it. Apparently, a view is clearly not to the viewer's credit, in the way a proper object of pride would be. Of course, it is possible to imagine being proud of having *created* a fine view (by careful planting and landscaping, perhaps), or of having *found* a wonderful view to show us (after a diligent search). But that is only to imagine being proud of something one has done, as we earlier imagined being proud of having completed a marathon. It is only to say once again that a person's actions can be to her credit, and thus proper sources of pride. The interesting question is whether anything *else* can be: are our actions and their outcomes the only legitimate sources of pride, so that being proud of anything else is like being proud of the view from the hillside?

Certainly, people do not, in fact, restrict their pride in that way. They are often proud of things that are not their doing, and that they do not even presume to be their doing. For example, a man might be proud of his good looks or handsome physique, without believing that he had created these as one might create a beautiful sculpture. He might regard them simply as good things about him, that is, and be proud of them on that basis. Similarly, someone who is proud of what her ancestors did need not think of their deeds as (somehow) her own. Instead, she might take their deeds to show what sort of person she is and be proud to be of such noble stock. To be proud she need not think of her noble stock as somehow her own doing—as, clearly, it is not—only that it is a distinguishing fact about her.

So it is certainly *possible* to take pride in something we have not done, to take it to speak well of us even so; the question is whether that sort of pride is inappropriate. Are we entitled to be proud of all our good points, or should we take pride only in that for which we bear some responsibility? I am inclined to take the latter view, and to think, therefore, that a humble person would not be proud of anything that was entirely a gift, but only of her actions and their results.

This would permit her to be proud of some of her traits and capacities, but only insofar as she had developed these herself. She could be proud of her self-control, for example, if this was something she had had to learn over time, or proud of her professional expertise or her skills as a cook. On the other hand, she would not be proud of anything with which she was *born*, so to speak. Nor would she take pride in anything she regarded as hers entirely through good fortune, unlike the man who is proud of his looks or the woman who is proud to be a Daughter of the American Revolution.

One reason to think it is wrong to be proud of what is not at all your doing is that such things are very like the view from the hillside, in an important respect. In both cases, you are only a beneficiary of some good thing: you have nothing more to do with it than that. That is what makes it so odd to be proud of the view from the hillside, I think: you are only in the right place at the right time for this to fall into your lap. If so, the same should apply to being proud of *anything* that you received only by chance. If your talent or your ancestry or your wealth came your way only by the luck of the draw, it would be equally inappropriate to be proud of them. You ought instead just to enjoy them and perhaps rejoice in your good luck, just as you might with the pleasant view.

To reinforce that conclusion, imagine someone who has won an enormous sum of money because his name was drawn at random from the telephone book. Unlike real life, suppose there is no catch: the money actually is his, and it is his un-conditionally. This delightful turn of events might please him greatly, of course, but suppose he were *proud* of it. Suppose he took his winning the money to be to his credit, in the way he might regard having acquired it through a carefully planned set of investments. This attitude would be so ludicrous that it is hard even to imagine. He would simply have no business being proud of his piece of good fortune, because he played no role in bringing it about.

A few of the good things about us are like that. It is very clear, if we give them a moment's thought, that they came our way entirely through agencies other than our own. People do sometimes take pride in such things even so, but their pride is as silly as that of the man we have just imagined. Take, for example, those who are proud to be descended from pioneers, or from Confederate soldiers. Obviously, that is not their doing, but entirely their good (or bad) luck. For them to be proud of it makes no more sense than it would for them to be *ashamed* of it: an attitude we would certainly think ill founded.

The great majority of the features of which we are proud are not this clear cut, however: how these features came to be facts about us is not so obvious. Perhaps they are partly our doing and thus legitimate sources of pride, and perhaps they are not. For example, it is hard to say whether certain basic intellectual skills and talents in the arts are products of genetics—whether they are "God-given," to put it in older language. Reasonable people disagree about the matter. It is also hard to say whether, for example, an especially sympathetic nature is acquired too early in life to count as the child's own doing, rather than as something largely to the credit of the child's parents. Accordingly, we cannot say that humility clearly precludes taking pride in these things: they may or may not be partly our own products.

The most we can say, it seems, is that humility precludes acting as if they were *entirely* our own doing, as if it were *purely* by dint of our own efforts that we were this bright or this capable or this sweet natured. For, that is plainly false; and, the pride one is due as a partial source of some good thing is not so great as that which a sole author would be entitled to take. Accordingly, humility ought at least to make us less proud of such things than some people seem to be, by keeping us aware that at most we are only partly responsible for them.

In the same way, humility would make us more modest than some seem to be in the pride they take in the accomplishments of their children. Humility would allow us to take some pride in our child's accomplishments, since we are partly responsible for the child's being the sort of person he or she is. And it would do nothing to diminish the delight we would take in the fact that this person we love is doing well. What humility would reduce is the degree to which we took the child's achievement to be to our credit. It would not allow the sort of pride in which parents act as if they had done the deed themselves, or as if the child were their robot.

For similar reasons, I think humility would also incline us away from the sort of pride that is competitive: the sort that amounts to being proud of having done better than others, rather than being proud of having done well. Since each of us acts within a context of other forces, the outcomes of our efforts are always only partly our doing, and partly the result of our luck in how these other forces act. To be aware of that is to recognize that doing better than someone else is often a matter simply of being luckier than she, and cannot be assumed to attest to one's own superiority. That means a humble person's pride would not typically be in having done better than others, but in having done well at whatever part he played.

These various points make it plain, at least, that a humble person would not be an overly proud one, in the sense of having exaggerated conceptions of his achievements and priding himself on matters with which he had little or nothing to do. To that extent the anitithesis between being proud and being humble is perfectly genuine. It holds, not because humility is a failure to appreciate oneself, however, but because humility limits that appreciation to occasions when it is justified. And it does therefore allow for pride, just as it allows for comfort despite opposing lavishness.

As a closing point concerning pride, notice that overweening pride comes in two distinct varieties, just as does the lack of self-respect that we sometimes mark by saying a person "has no pride." When we think of someone who "has no pride," it is natural to picture him as demoting only himself:

as taking himself to be *uniquely* worthless, for reasons he is not good at articulating. There is also a second way of lacking self-respect, though, in which a person thinks badly of herself because she is "only a woman," for example, or because she is black, or because she is working class. She lacks respect not only for herself but for all who share what she takes to be the stigma.

Similarly, we may be inclined at first to picture those who lack humility as elevating only *themselves*. Such a person does not believe there is anyone quite like his wonderful self, in somewhat the same way as someone who feels worthless might believe there is no one else as worthless as his undeserving self. Just as there is a second way to lack self-respect, though, there should also be a second way to lack humility. A lack of humility would involve taking oneself to be a member of an elite, *all* of whom one would acknowledge to be superior to the hoipolloi. Not that the other members of the elite would be much on this person's mind, necessarily. But if pressed, he would agree that everyone who belongs to *the club* is a superior human being. The point is that he need not think only he is so grand, for this to be a failure of humility.

It *is* necessary that his elitist confidence be quite unwarranted, however. For, it is possible to overestimate our position innocently rather than arrogantly, as noted in Chapter 5. A new member of the faculty might believe herself entitled to a special discount at the campus bookstore, for example, because that was the arrangement at her previous college. If she is wrong about that, she is taking herself to have privileges that ordinary folk do not. This would not be arrogance on her part, though, because her mistake is not an unreasonable one. It is not as if she believed her faculty status entitled her to treat the secretary as a personal servant, or made her a better human being than all those who work outside the ivory tower. Elitism, like most arrogance, is easier to sustain if we give no

thought to the principles we are enacting; once a person for-
mulates them as principles, it is hard not to see them as ludicrous.

Freedom from elitism is among the advantages of humility, then. There are many others. A person who does not overestimate his abilities is less likely to undertake projects that
are beyond him, or to fret impatiently when difficult tasks are
not easily completed. There is protection here as well against
frustration over lost competitions, derived from a good sense
as to when we simply would not be in the running and so
ought not to feel sure someone must have cheated or to reproach ourselves for not having done better. A humble person
is free to admire rather than to envy or to burn in some other
way.

As another part of understanding themselves, the humble
are aware that they do not necessarily know what course
would be in another person's best interests. This alone should
make them cautious about pressing their unwanted expertise
upon others—to be bewildered, sometimes, by its rejection.
By the same token, to understand ourselves is to know better
than to think we are nothing, that others may treat us as they
wish or that we must allow them to make the decisions that
shape our lives. Having self-respect in this way is not what we
think of as an *expression* of humility, but the two have a natural connection.

Although humility involves having a sense of one's worth,
it also acquaints a person with the fact that she is not *uniquely*
worthy. She will know she is not so important to the universe
as she is to herself: although she may be first in her own heart,
she will not take it that others must somehow *err* by having
different priorities. That may seem an obvious thing to know,
but many seem not to know it. To live in accordance with the
knowledge that you are not uniquely important enhances the
ability to manage the mistreatment you suffer, rather than having it disrupt your life out of all proportion. To live in accordance with this knowledge enhances the ability to tolerate

minor human error when it affects you, as opposed to considering everytime you are wronged so outrageous that all must take notice and the miscreant must be made to suffer. To know you are not uniquely important makes extending forgiveness a possibility, by enabling you to see that not every time you are wronged has the status of a sacrilege.

On the other hand, to know that you have no unique intrinsic importance is to know that others are entitled to take their mistreatment every bit as seriously as you are entitled to take yours. What is more, others are entitled to the same concern about their mistreatment from the rest of the world as well. This should mean recognizing that you must take some care regarding others, insofar as you feel entitled to have them take care regarding you. Indeed, you should see that the more intimate your relationship with others the greater they merit your concern. For, the more intimate the relationship, the more concern you feel entitled to expect from them. The even-handedness of humility's perspective thus removes one obstacle to intimacy, as well as erasing more generally the self-aggrandizement of the egotist.

Nor will anyone who knows herself be greatly self-absorbed, for she will see that she is not so much more fascinating than other subjects. That will free her to be compassionate, among other things, without of course meaning that she must take no greater interest in herself than she takes in remote strangers. It means instead that she will be distractable from self-interested pursuits, that her heart will not be entirely closed.

Martin Luther once asserted that humility is so wonderful a virtue that one can never be aware of having it, for the awareness would surely turn one's head. I doubt the advantages cited above are quite so dazzling as that. They do seem, however, to make humility both a valuable asset to the person who has it and something we should welcome in those who cross our path. Being humble is a good way for a person to be.

NOTES

Introduction

1. "True humility, therefore, never knows that it is humble, as I have said; for if it knew this, it would turn proud from contemplation of so fine a virtue." Martin Luther, "*The Sermon on the Mount*" *and "The Magnificat,"* vol. 21 of *Luther's Works*, trans. and ed. Jaroslav Pelikan (St. Louis: Concordia, 1956), p. 315.
2. See Jeffrie G. Murphy, "Forgiveness and Resentment," in *Social and Political Philosophy*, ed. Peter A. French, Theodore E. Uehling, Jr., and Howard K. Wettstein, vol. 7 of Midwest Studies in Philosophy (Minneapolis: University of Minnesota Press, 1982), pp. 503–16, and Jeffrie G. Murphy and Jean Hampton, *Forgiveness and Mercy* (Cambridge: Cambridge University Press, 1988).

Chapter 1

1. Henry Sidgwick, *The Methods of Ethics* [1874], 7th ed. (Chicago: University of Chicago Press, 1962), p. 334.
2. Bernard of Clairvaux, Sermon 42 on Canticle 6, as translated by George Bosworth Burch in his Introduction to Bernard's *The Steps of Humility*, trans. George Bosworth Burch (Cambridge, Mass.: Harvard University Press, 1942), p. 51.
3. Martin Luther, *Devotional Writings I*, vol. 42 of *Luther's Works*, trans. and ed. Jaroslav Pelikan (St. Louis: Concordia, 1956), p. 70.
4. Sidgwick, *Methods of Ethics*, p. 335.
5. Gabriele Taylor, *Pride, Shame and Guilt* (Oxford: Clarendon Press, 1985), p. 17.
6. Aurel Kolnai, "Dignity," *Philosophy* 51 (1976): 253.
7. Bernard of Clairvaux, *Steps of Humility*, p. 205.
8. I am grateful to Bruce Kimball for this suggestion.
9. Bernard of Clairvaux, *Steps of Humility*, p. 247.
10. Jeffrie G. Murphy, "Forgiveness and Resentment," in *Social and*

Political Philosophy, ed. Peter A. French, Theodore E. Uehling, Jr., and Howard K. Wettstein, vol. 7 of Midwest Studies in Philosophy (Minneapolis: University of Minnesota Press, 1982), p. 505.

Chapter 2

1. Jeffrie Murphy makes the points just mentioned, in the course of arguing that to abandon hard feelings for the reasons cited is not actually to *forgive* at all. See his "Forgiveness and Resentment," in *Social and Political Philosophy*, ed. Peter A. French, Theodore E. Uehling, Jr., and Howard K. Wittstein, vol. 7 of Midwest Studies in Philosophy (Minneapolis: University of Minnesota Press, 1982), and a later version included under the same title in Jeffrie G. Murphy and Jean Hampton, *Forgiveness and Mercy* (Cambridge: Cambridge University Press, 1988).
2. Jeffrie G. Murphy, "Forgiveness and Resentment," in *Forgiveness and Mercy*, p. 16, his emphasis. All references will be to this version of Murphy's views, since it is the more recent; all emphases are his.
3. Ibid., p. 17.
4. Ibid., p. 25.
5. Ibid., p. 28.
6. Ibid., p. 26.
7. Ernest Hemingway, *The Sun Also Rises* (New York: Charles Scribner's Sons, 1926), pp. 48–51. See p. 194 for his description of Jake as "the only friend I had."
8. Ibid., pp. 141–42, 177.
9. Ibid., p. 194.
10. Murphy, "Forgiveness and Resentment," p. 18.
11. Henry James, *The Portrait of a Lady* (1881; reprint, New York: Random House, 1951), 1:217.
12. Ibid., p. 121.
13. Murphy, "Forgiveness and Resentment," p. 18.
14. Joseph Butler, "Upon Forgiveness of Injuries," in *The Works of the Right Reverend Father in God, Joseph Butler, D.C.L., Late Bishop of Durham*, ed. Samuel Halifax (New York: Carter, 1846), p. 110.
15. Ibid., p. 111.
16. There is another possibility. Suppose our man knows perfectly well that he can never achieve the standards he sets for himself, but truly does set himself those. He does chastise himself for his

failures, that is, even though he does not believe he could have done any better. Such a person is not lacking in humility, although he does seem to be deeply unfair to himself.

Chapter 3

1. Peter Singer, "Rich and Poor," in *Practical Ethics* (Cambridge: Cambridge University Press, 1979), p. 169. See also his "Famine, Affluence, and Morality," *Philosophy and Public Affairs* 1 (1971–72): 229–41.
2. Singer, "Rich and Poor," p. 159.
3. "Famine," *Time*, December 21, 1987, p. 35.
4. Ibid.
5. John W. Miller and Sarah Gavian, "Famine: Causes, Prevention, and Relief," *Science* 235 (January 30, 1987): 543.
6. The advertisements run regularly. See, for example, *New Yorker*, May 7, 1989, pp. 3, 83.
7. "Famine," *Time*, p. 35.
8. See P. F. Strawson, "Freedom and Resentment," *Proceedings of the British Academy* 48 (1962): 1–25.
9. Lawrence Blum, "Compassion," in *Explaining Emotions*, ed. Amelie Oksenberg Rorty (Berkeley and Los Angeles: University of California Press, 1980), p. 508.
10. According to Bishop Butler, Thomas Hobbes did take compassion to consist in taking someone's troubles as a warning for one's own future conduct. See Butler's sermon "Upon Compassion," in *The Works of the Right Reverend Father in God, Joseph Butler, D.C.L., Late Bishop of Durham*, ed. Samuel Halifax (New York: Carter, 1846), p. 64.
11. Blum, "Compassion," p. 513.
12. "My context for this inquiry is an interest in developing an alternative to Kantianism, in particular to its minimization of the role of emotion in morality and its exclusive emphasis on duty and rationality." (Ibid., p. 507.) Richard Taylor undertakes the same project in "The Virtue of Compassion," in *Good and Evil* (New York: Macmillan, 1970), pp. 205–22.
13. Perhaps more surprisingly, neither does he have any interest in compassion. That concept is never deployed. Singer's argument is not that a good heart calls for us to change our ways, but that reason does: essentially, that our way of life awards significance to irrelevant differences.

14. The quotation is from Singer's "Famine, Affluence, and Morality," p. 174. His "Rich and Poor" contains a version of the same claim that distance is irrelevant, p. 171.

15. Samuel Scheffler also objects to the idea that our own fortunes should count no more with us than those of others, on the ground that this alienates us from our own projects and undermines our integrity. See *The Rejection of Consequentialism* (Oxford: Clarendon Press, 1984), esp. pp. 7–10, 12–16, and 37–60 *passim*.

16. Singer, "Rich and Poor," p. 158.

17. The example is Ludwig Wittgenstein's. See *Philosophical Investigations*, trans. G.E.M. Anscombe (Oxford: Basil Blackwell, 1963), p. 174e.

18. For a complete discussion of this idea, see Robert E. Goodin, *Protecting the Vulnerable* (Chicago and London: University of Chicago Press, 1985).

19. Again, this is offered, not as a criticism of Singer, but as a view I have constructed about what humility requires.

20. See James Rachels, *The End of Life* (Oxford: Oxford University Press, 1986), pp. 134–39.

Chapter 4

1. Joseph Butler, "Upon Compassion," in *The Works of the Right Reverend Father in God, Joseph Butler, D.C.L., Late Bishop of Durham*, ed. Samuel Halifax (New York: Carter, 1846), p. 66. Butler devoted two sermons to the topic, each beginning from the verse quoted.

2. Butler believed it would be a wonderful thing if we were less discriminating in the people with whom we rejoice. That would add a lot of happiness to our lives at no apparent cost to us, he observed, whereas feeling sorry for those in trouble and trying to help them can be quite costly. What intrigued Butler was why God did not make us that way, instead of making us rather uninterested in those who are doing well.

3. Daniel Farrell, "Jealousy," *Philosophical Review*, October 1980, p. 532. See also Leslie H. Farber, "Faces of Envy," in *The Virtues*, ed. Robert B. Kruschwitz and Robert C. Roberts (Belmont, Calif.: Wadsworth, 1987), pp. 168–70.

4. Thomas Aquinas, *Summa Theologica*, trans. Fathers of the English Dominican Province (New York: Benziger Brothers, 1947), pt. II–II, ques. 36, art. 4.

5. Ibid., art. 3.

6. Dante Alighieri, *The Divine Comedy*, *Purgatory*, Canto XIII, trans. Henry Francis Cary (New York: P. F. Collier and Son, 1901), pp. 193–97.

7. Although Farrell mentions only friendly *envy*, we use "I am so *jealous*" and even "I *hate* you" as the same hyperbole to say, roughly, that you have something so wonderful that it could inspire such feelings in a person of a certain kind. It is not really hatred we are expressing, nor is it genuine jealousy or envy.

   Gabriele Taylor's caution about friendly envy applies to all of these: she observes that even the admiration they express can be a bad thing in its own way, depending on "how domineering the image of the admired person may become in the other's life." Gabriele Taylor, "Envy and Jealousy: Emotions and Vices," in *Ethical Theory: Character and Virtue*, ed. Peter A. French, Theodore E. Uehling, Jr., and Howard K. Wettstein, vol. 13 of Midwest Studies in Philosophy (Notre Dame: Notre Dame University Press, 1988), p. 234.

8. Here too I follow Farrell. For his version of this idea see "Of Jealousy and Envy," in *Person to Person*, ed. George Graham and Hugh LaFollette (Philadelphia: Temple University Press, 1989), p. 253.

9. Here I depart from Farrell, who considers it sufficient to say that in envy "we are in fact *bothered*, however mildly, by the fact that they have what we want but do not have." ("Of Jealousy and Envy," p. 254.) The trouble is that there is more than one way to be bothered by that fact. It can make you wistful or depressed, for example, without also making you envious, if it makes you think only of your failures and not (enviously) of the other person's successes. Hence I think it necessary to say that in envy the person's having what you lack not only bothers you but affects your feelings toward him or her.

10. This second strategy is nicely sketched in Farber, "Faces of Envy."

11. Of course, it is also possible to envy someone you hate. That would be expressed by your being upset both by his doing well and by his doing better than you, on the present account.

12. One version of this argument is to be found in Farrell, "Jealousy," p. 547, another in his "Of Jealousy and Envy," pp. 256–57.

13. This is offered purely as a way of thinking about baseless jealousy, not as a daring piece of Shakespearean scholarship revealing the right way to read the play.

14. That was not entirely foolish of us, if Laurence Thomas is

right in arguing that to have more than one close friend is very difficult. See his *Living Morally* (Philadelphia: Temple University Press, 1989), pp. 111–14. Thomas credits this idea to Aristotle.

15. Thomas Aquinas, *Summa Theologica*, pt. II–II, ques. 36, art. 1.
16. Cicero, *Tusculan Disputations*, with an Eng. trans. by J. E. King (Cambridge, Mass.: Harvard University Press, 1981), 4.8. I am grateful to George McClure for providing this reference.
17. Ibid.
18. Aristotle, *Rhetoric*, trans. Lane Cooper (New York: Appleton-Century, 1932), 2.1388b (parentheses are the translator's).
19. Ibid., 1388a. It only "makes for envy" when our reaction includes some negative feelings about those we envy, I have claimed.

Chapter 5

1. Joel Feinberg, *Harm to Self* (Oxford: Oxford University Press, 1986), p. 25. See pp. 52–57 for an intriguing exploration of the analogy between national sovereignty and personal autonomy.
2. This is adapted from an episode in Marcel Ophul's film *The Sorrow and the Pity*. There, two former heroes of the resistance are asked what caused them to lead such dangerous lives under the occupation. We might expect to hear about *La belle France* or loyalty to fallen comrades or at least about some stirring call issued by General De Gaulle. Instead, they say that one day in their local bakery Nazi soldiers pushed to the front of the line and demanded immediate service—and that was enough!
3. Lady Hamilton provided some encouragement of her own, of course: "He had meant to stay at Naples only a short time. But the Hamiltons were making him extremely comfortable, and his hostess, younger than himself, was a strikingly beautiful and fascinating woman who plied him with flattery, of which he never seemed to tire. Nor did he dislike being the lion of Neapolitan society and the honoured adviser of the King and Queen, who regarded him as their saviour and defender." (Captain Russell Greenfell, R.N., *Nelson the Sailor* [New York: Macmillan, 1950], pp. 110–11.) Even those who consider their affair chiefly Lady Hamilton's doing acknowledge the extent to which Nelson had grown arrogant: "Within three days he had been persuaded that upon his personal presence depended the salvation of Italy. . . . The current (of praise) was swollen to a torrent by the streams of adulation, which from all quarters flowed in upon a temperament only too disposed to

accept them. . . . Within a week the conviction of his own importance led him to write to Lady Hamilton, evidently for transmis-
sion to the Queen, an opinion, or rather an urgent expression of
advice, that Naples should at once begin war. . . . There is no record of any official request for this unofficial and irregular com-
munication of the opinion of a British admiral." (Captain A. T.
Mahan, *The Life of Nelson, the Embodiment of the Power of Great
Britain* [1897; reprint, New York: Greenwood Press, 1968], 1:388–
90.)

4. Henry James, *The Portrait of a Lady* (1881; reprint, New York:
   Random House, 1951), 1:344–45.
5. John Stuart Mill, *On Liberty*, in *The Utilitarians* (Garden City,
   N.Y.: Anchor Books, 1973), p. 560.
6. Ibid., p. 484.
7. Ibid., p. 553.
8. Feinberg, *Harm to Self*, all quotations from p. 12.
9. See ibid., esp. pp. 23, 25–26.

Chapter 6

1. John Stuart Mill, *On Liberty*, in *The Utilitarians* (Garden City,
   N.Y.: Anchor Books, 1973), p. 553.
2. Bruce L. Miller, "Autonomy and the Refusal of Lifesaving Treatment," in *Ethical Issues in Modern Medicine*, ed. John Arras and
   Nancy Rhoden, 3d ed. (Mountain View, Calif.: Mayfield Publish-
   ing Company, 1989), p. 168. Miller notes that the case is drawn
   from Eric J. Cassell, "The Function of Medicine," *Hastings Center
   Report* 6 (1976): 16.
3. Perhaps it assumes that incompetence includes an inability to
   guide one's life according to one's desires; if so, to say the incompetent have the usual authority to do that very thing does seem
   pretty silly. This rationale for the position, however, owes us an
   account of guiding one's life according to one's desires. Its de-
   fenders must also cope with the suspicion that many of those we
   consider incompetent are *not* unable to pursue their desires but
   simply have desires that strike the rest of us as bizarre, or sets of
   desires we consider improper in their relative intensities. If that
   suspicion is sound, we shall need a different justification for denying the incompetent the authority to live as they wish.
4. John Locke, *An Essay Concerning the True Original, Extent, and
   End of Civil Government*, in *The English Philosophers from Ba-
   con to Mill*, ed. Edwin A. Burtt (New York: Random House,

1939), p. 413. The essay is commonly known as Locke's *Second Treatise on Government*; the quotation is from chap. 5, par. 3.

5. James Rachels, *The End of Life* (Oxford: Oxford University Press, 1986), p. 65.

6. See, for example, Lawrence Becker, *Property Rights* (London: Routledge and Kegan Paul, 1977). Following A. M. Honoré, Becker lists among eleven elements of full ownership "the right to the capital—that is, the power to alienate the thing and to consume, waste, modify, or destroy it" (p. 19). According to Becker, "The right to the capital is the only one of the elements which seems able to define a variety of ownership standing alone. It is the most fundamental of the elements, if only because it includes the right to destroy, consume, and alienate" (p. 20).

7. Rachels, *End of Life*, p. 71.

8. John Barth, *The End of the Road*, rev. ed. (Garden City, N.Y.: Doubleday, 1962), p. 83.

9. Charles Dickens, *The Personal History of David Copperfield* (New York: Grosset & Dunlop, 1931), p. 1.

10. Ronald Dworkin, "The Rights of Allan Bakke," in *Morality and Moral Controversies*, ed. John Arthur, 2d ed. (Englewood Cliffs, N.J.: Prentice-Hall, 1986), p. 332.

Chapter 7

1. Henry David Thoreau, *Walden*, Modern Library (New York: Random House, 1937), p. 60.

2. Ibid., pp. 292–93.

3. Ibid., p. 293.

4. Thomas Aquinas, *Summa Theologica*, trans. Fathers of the English Dominican Province (New York: Benziger Brothers, 1947), pt. II–II, ques. 161, art. 3.

5. G. A. Gilleman, "Humility," *New Catholic Encyclopedia* (New York: McGraw-Hill, 1967), 7:235.

6. Ibid., p. 236.

7. Ignatius Loyola, *The Spiritual Exercises of St. Ignatius Loyola*, trans. "A Benedictine of Stanbrook," ed. the Reverend E. Lattey, S.J. (St. Louis and London: B. Herder Book Company, 1928), p. 30. Ignatius Loyola founded the Jesuit order.

8. Thomas à Kempis, *The Imitation of Christ*, trans. (1530) Richard Whitford, ed. Edward J. Klein (New York and London: Harper and Brothers, 1941), p. 39.

9. Loyola, *Spiritual Exercises*, p. 38.

10. Ibid., p. 39.

11. Thomas Aquinas, *Summa Theologica*, pt. II–II, ques. 161, art. 5.
12. Loyola, *Spiritual Exercises*, p. 32. See also Thomas à Kempis, *Imitation of Christ*, esp. pp. 17–21.
13. Donald B. Kraybill, *The Riddle of Amish Culture* (Baltimore: Johns Hopkins University Press, 1989), p. 41.
14. To appreciate this argument, keep in mind that the Amish know what each other are doing, and that no one is supposed to act remarkably differently than anyone else: allowing one person his innovation requires allowing its general spread. Then consider these remarks about shifting from farming with horses to farming with tractors: "We farm with horses, so that we're satisfied with eighty acres of land, where a Mennonite, hey, he can't afford to pay $40,000 for a tractor and only farm eighty acres. He's got to farm half the neighborhood to make it pay. Then he needs some bigger equipment, he needs a combine, and then he needs the whole bit." (Ibid., p. 91.) "If we allowed tractors, we would be doing like the Mennonite people are doing, grabbing each other's farms up out there, mechanizing, and going to the bank and loaning [sic] $500,000 and worrying about later paying it off, putting three other guys out of business and sending them to town for work, away from their home." (Ibid., p. 239.)
15. Ibid., p. 41–45.
16. Thomas Aquinas, *Summa Theologica*, pt. II–II, ques. 36, art. 1: "Another's good may be reckoned as being one's own evil, in so far as it conduces to the lessening of one's own good name or excellence. It is in this way that envy grieves for another's good: and consequently men are envious of those goods in which a good name consists, and about which men like to be honored and esteemed."
17. Ibid., ques. 161, art. 2.
18. I do not mean to suggest that Aquinas would have given this same account of why humility and boasting are incongruent.
19. Kraybill, *Riddle of Amish Culture*, p. 29.
20. Ibid., p. 30.
21. Ibid., p. 25.
22. Ibid.
23. Ibid., p. 36.

Chapter 8

1. Peter Singer, "Famine, Affluence, and Morality," *Philosophy and Public Affairs* 1 (1971–72): 229–41.

2. As I point out in Chapter 7, humility also makes a person averse to certain lavish and self-absorbed styles of life, and to pressing one's material success upon the notice of others. It would follow that a humble person would not be made envious by the spectacle of someone living in those ways. He might envy the wealthy the ease in their lives, compared to his own harder way, but that is something different. Moreover, his envy might be diminished too by his recognition that there is no competition here in which he is falling behind, and no injury done him by the wealthy person's having an easy life.
3. Richard Taylor, *Virtue Ethics* (Interlaken, N.Y.: Linden Books, 1991), p. 99.

INDEX